YATINDRA MATA DIPIKA

OR

LIGHT OF THE SCHOOL

OF

SRI RAMANUJA

YATINDRA MATA DIPIKA

OR

LIGHT OF THE SCHOOL

OF

SRI RAMANUJA

SRINIVASA-TRANSLATOR-GOVINDA
CARYA SVAMIN

Published by

FacsiMile Publisher
12 Pragati Market
Ashok Vihar, Ph-2
Delhi - 110052, India
Phone: 011-47034999
Email: www.facsimilepublishers.com
info@facsimilepublishers.com

Distribution Network
gyanbooks.com
India, USA, Canada, UK, Australia

ISBN: 978-93-7106-246-6 (PB)

First Published, 1912

2nd Impression 2025

Printed at: Gyan Press, Delhi.

YATINDRA MATA DIPIKA OR LIGHT OF THE SCHOOL OF SRI RAMANUJA

Arthur SRINIVASA-TRANSLATOR-GOVINDA CARYA SVAMIN

YATINDRA - MATA - DIPIKA

Or The Light Of The School Of Sri Ramanuja

Srinivasa, A. Govinda - Carya Svamin(Tr.)

Yatindra-Mata-Dipika

OR

THE LIGHT OF THE SCHOOL

OF

SRI RAMANUJA

BY

SRINIVĀSA

TRANSLATED INTO ENGLISH WITH NOTES ETC.,

BY

A. GOVINDA- CARYA SVAMIN, C.E; M.R.A.S; M.R.S.A; ETC.

AUTHOR OF VARIOUS WORKS.

MADRAS

AT THE MEYKANḌĀN PRESS

1912

Works* by the same Author—*In English.*

		Rs.	A.	P.
1.	Bhagavad-gītā with Rāmānuja's commentaries...	5	0	0
2.	Lives of the Drāviḍa Saints (Āzhvârs).	1	8	0
3.	Lives of Rāmānuja and other Sages (with frontispiece etc.)...	2	12	0
4.	Divine Wisdom of the Drāviḍa Saints.	2	0	0
5.	Vade-Mecum of Vedānta ...	1	0	0
6.	Artha-Pañçaka or Five Truths (JRAS)	0	12	0
7.	Vedānta and Theosophy ...	0	4	6
8.	Three Parts: Lectures on Inspiration, Intuition and Ecstacy...	1	0	0
9.	Ideals of Ind, in Two Parts ...	0	12	0
10.	Yatīndra-Mata-Dīpikā (or a Compendium of Viśishṭâdvaita Philosophy and Religion			
11.	Other Contributions to the Journal of the Royal Asiatic Society, Indian Antiquary, Siddhānta Dīpikā etc., etc., ...			

* [*Obtainable at Veda-Gṛham, 1050, Viceroy Road, Mysore, South India or from the Publisher, the "Siddhānta Dīpikā" Choolai, Madras, N.C.*]

D

IN MEMORY

OF THE VISIT OF

THEIR IMPERIAL MAJESTIES

King George V and Queen Mary

CROWNED IN DEHLI, INDIA,

AS

EMPEROR & EMPRESS OF INDIA

ON THE 12TH DECEMBER 1911.

CONTENTS.

Frontispiece A. GOVINDÂCĀRYA SVĀMIN.

N.B.—The Scheme of Transliteration is that adopted by the Royal Asiatic Society of Great Britain and Ireland (JRAS,) except *sh*. Brahma-sūtras = Vedānta-sūtras. *It* or *He* are both used for God and Soul. And *She* also, were it used, would, for Saṁskṛt, mean the same. The gender is inconsequential.

PREFACE.

THE appearance of this work was adumbrated in the Artha-Pañcaka or The "Five Truths", in the pages of the JRAS (Journal of the Royal Asiatic Society), p. 565, July 1910. It was to have appeared in the same Journal, but for paucity of space for a work extending over more than 45 pages. It was decided therefore to bring out an independent edition in India, which, as a book of reference for all time on the Viśishṭâ-'dvaita Philosophy and Religion, is expected to be more accommodating to the general reader than if it appeared in an academic Journal inaccessible to all. Being an academic work itself, the printing of it in *propria forma* demanded by the exigencies of Saṁskṛta orthography, was made possible by the Meykaṇḍān Press, under the supervision of its intelligent proprietor Mr. J. N. Rāmanāthan, of Madras, undertaking to meet all the requirements incidental to such a work. It is hoped the readers will find the justness of my remarks when they may come to examine it for themselves.

2. In the shape of introduction to the work, very little need be written, it seems to me, inasmuch

as scholars are more in need of original matter than attempts made at theses for which there seems at present no warranty. But if a popular introduction were yet deemed necessary, my work called the *Vade Mecum of Vedānta* affords an appropriate pourparler to the *Yatīndra-Mata-Dīpikā*,—the work which, with this preface, makes its debut into the arena of Indology. The necessity also for such preliminaries is as far as possible obviated by the copious foot-notes which will be found sprinkled in sufficient profusion, in almost every page, not only to elucidate the abstruse subject-matter but as well to reduce to the utmost minimum the jejune nature which is a *sine qua non* of all academic studies,—the Oriental in a large measure. The desideratum for a separate glossary of technical terms which by necessity teem in all works of an academic nature,. is met by the scheme, adopted in this work, of inditing all such terms side by side their English, in brackets or otherwise. Facilities for comprehension are better afforded, I trust, by this mode than if they had to be procured by constant references to a glossary at the sacrifice of time, with mental poise liable to be ruffled by such a process of glossarial interference, at every step of a perusal. Strictest fidelity to the original Saṁskṛta might, it is feared, have led to the English rendering being found stiff and in places lacking, peradventure, in clarity. But this is due more to the technical nature of the subject than to any perfunctoriness on the part of the translator, who is conscious of having done his best. The subject itself is rigid, and invites the mental concentration of the student, not the surface-skimming of the light reader.

3. With regard to the author of *Yatindra-Mata-Dipikā*, Šrinivāsa, we learn from the invocatory verses (left untranslated), where mention of Mahâ-"cārya in the preliminary of Advent I, synonymously referred to again as Ghana-guru-vara in the Colophon is made, that he, (viz., Šrinivāsa) is the immediate disciple of Doḍḍay-ārya, which is the colloquial of Mahâ-"ārya which is the same as Mahâ-"cārya. There is a succession of apostles of the Rāmānuja School beginning from Dāšarathi or Mudaliy-āṇḍān, Šri-Rāmānuja's sister's son *, famed as of the *Kandāḍai* descent. To this stem belong all the Mahâ-"cāryas, a branch—an important one—settling down at Ghaṭikâ-'cala, otherwise known as Choḷa-simhapuram (vulgarised as Sholinghur,—a station on the Railway track linking Bangalūr and Madras), which is referred to by Šrinivāsa, the author of Yatindra-Mata-Dipikā, as Ghaṭikâ-"dri, in his invocatory verse to the work. This place is a noted shrine, very ancient as having been sung by the archaic Āzhvārs or Drāviḍa Saints

* See (my) *Life of Rāmānuja* etc.

in their Tamiḻ Works the *Prabandhas* * ;—Nṛsiṁha, one of the Ten Avatāras of Vishṇu being the presiding Deity of the place. One of the Mahâ-"cāryas is noted in history as Caṇḍa-māruta Mahâ-"cārya by reason of a great polemical work called Caṇḍa-māruta (=hurricane) having been written by him on an anterior work the Ŝata-dūshaṇī of a similar character, composed by the great Vedāntâ-"cārya [1268 A.C. born], who is the contemporary of Mādhava or Vidyāraṇya [1331 A.C. elected for Ŝṛṅgeri pontificate, in the now Mysore State]. The author mentions (in the Conclusion-Chapter) both these works among others as those on which he bases his compendium of Viŝishṭâ-'dvaita Vedānta, viz., the *Yatīndra-Mata-Dīpikā*. Hence it may be reasonably conjectured that Ŝrīnivāsa is the immediate disciple of Ghaṭikâ-'cala Caṇḍamāruta Mahâ-"cārya. This Mahâ-"cārya is a contemporary of Appaya-Dīkshita, who is a commentator on Vedāntâ-"cārya's works. A tradition in currency further confirms this contemporaneity, which may be cited here, in almost the words kindly supplied me by my valued friend Ŝrī M. T. Narasiṁha-iyaṅgār, B.A., M.R.A.S., Professor in the Central College, Bangalūr:—

"These two authors, Mahâ-"cārya and Appaya-Dīkshita were close friends, both being the

---

* *Vide* (my) *Lives of Saints.*

unparalleled Vidvāns of the age; and they used to discuss philosophical questions very often, with a view to try their own skill in argument. Both were admirers of Vedāntâ-"cārya, whose works they commented largely. Appaya-Dikshita, as is well-known to all Saṁskṛt scholars, was a staunch devotee of Šiva,* in spite of his having devoted his time to writing commentaries on the Višishṭâ-"dvaitic works of Vedāntâ-"cārya, and he wanted to construe the term Nārāyaṇa as applicable to his favourite deity Šiva. Mahâ-"cārya, seeing that his friend attempted a point (for argument) that could not at all be maintained on *grammatical basis* (*at most*) waited for an opportunity to test the truth of his friend's conviction on the point in question. Once when they were both getting up the Aḻagar-malai about eight miles from Madura, (on which the temple of *Sundara-bāhu* or *Aḻagar* is situate, and where

* Cp, the verse which no is alleged to have been uttered by him in a meeting of Paṇḍits at Kāñcipura:

Mahešvare vā jagatām adhīšvare
Janārdane vā jagad-antar-ātmani
Na vastu-bheda-pratipattir asti me
Tathâ-'pi bhaktis Taruṇ-endu-šekhare.

The gist of the verse is that he saw no distinction between Šiva and Vishṇu, yet he had a penchant for Šiva. See foot-note 238, page 116. [A. G.]

the famous Nūpura-gaṅgā rill runs), Mahâ-"cārya took advantage of a position when he could extract the truth of his friend's conviction on the disputed point from his own mouth. Among the initial steps leading to the temple of *Sundara-bāhu*, the eighteenth step from the bottom is regarded as presided over by a *bhūta* (spirit) named in Tamiḻ *Karappān*; and the belief was that whoever speaks untruth (or proves false) while on this step, would suffer instantaneous death. (It is for this reason that the temple-keys used to be left, during nights, on this step, without any fear of thieves touching them). (Here) Mahâ-"cārya took hold of his friend's hand and making him stand there, questioned him thus;—"Tell me, my dear friend! are you really convinced that the term Nārāyaṇa can be construed as a name of Śiva? I ask you now because you cannot speak untruth *here*, for the sake of argument!" Then Appaya-Dikshita is said to have spoken out his own conviction to this effect;—'The letter Ṇ (ण) in the term Nārāyaṇa is in the way of such construction. This is my conviction.' * "

* Appaya-Dikshita accedes to this confession, beyond grammatical reasons merely, in his commentary on verse 35 of *Ānanda-laharī* [Pp. 64-65.]

This great Appaya-Dīkshita's date is correctly known as 1552—1624 A.C. as proved by various evidences such as (1) his living at Vellore, under the patronage of Chinna Bomma Bhūpāla, (2) his being invited to the court of the Penukoṇḍa ruler Veṅkaṭa-deva (1586—1613 A.C); (3) his being the Vedānta teacher of the great grammarian Bhaṭṭoji-Dīkshita,

---

edited by R. Hālāsyanātha Śāstrin, 1908. [*Vāṇī-vilāsa Press*, Śrīraṅgam] thus:—

'Veda-vibhāgâ-'rtham evâ 'vatīrṇena sakala-Veda-tātparyâ-'bhijñena sarvajña-śikhāmaṇinā bhagavatā Veda-Vyāsena, Pulastya-vara-dāna-labdha-devatā-pāram-ārthya-vedanena Śrī-Parāśareṇâ, 'nyais ca maharshibhir Ved-opa-bṛhmaṇâ-'rtham praṇīteshu Śrī Mahābhārata-Vishṇu-Purāṇâ-"dishu, niścita-Parabrahma-bhāvasya, sadbhis sarvair apy avibhā-gena Para-Brahm-ety eva pūjitasya *Śrī-Nārāyaṇasya*, kvacit-koṇe-nivishṭa-mantrâ-"rthavāda-purāṇa-vaca-nâ-"dileśam avalambya jīvabhāvam vaktum nâ 'smaj-jihvā pravartate, tathā cen mūrdhā ca śatadhā bhavati; Veda-Vaidika-droho, Devatā-drohaś ca jāyate. Ato *Nārayaṇaḥ* Para-Brahma-kotir ity evâ 'asmākam siddhāntaḥ.'

The gist of this passage is that his head will shatter into hundreds of fragments if he dared to gainsay the verdict of all the great Sages Vyāsa, Parāśara etc., about Nārāyaṇa being the Great God, in all their authoritative works; that he dare not commit such heresy and blasphemy. [A. G.]

(4) his antagonism with the famous poet Jagannātha Paṇḍita or Paṇḍita-rāya, the author of *Citra-mīmāṁsā-khaṇḍana*, etc.

We can therefore conclude that Mahâ-"cārya (who by tradition was equally old with Appaya-Dīkshita, while the Aḷagar-malai incident took place, as chronicled above) lived in the latter part of the 16th and the beginning of the 17th centuries. Our author Śrīnivāsa therefore, who is the son of Svāmi-pushkariṇī Govindâ-"rya,—servitor at the Holy Hill Veṅkaṭa-giri (Tirupati)—and disciple of Mahâ-"cārya, may be placed at the beginning of the 17th century.

4. This author of Yatīndra-Mata-Dīpikā had, according to the invocatory verse, a vision where he saw Veṅkaṭeśa (the God of Tirupati), Devarāja (the God of Kariśaila = Kāñcī), Nṛsiṁha (the God of Ghaṭikâ-"dri), along with Kṛshṇa (= Yāmunâ-"cārya) and Yatirāja (= Rāmānuja), and that seems to be the inspiration quickening him to the composition of an authoritative text-book, embodying in it all the quintessence of the doctrines of Visishṭâ-dvaita Philosophy and Religion promulgated by Śrī Rāmānuja, which he fitly titles as the; YATĪNDRA MATA-DĪPIKĀ or The Light of the School of Rāmānuja.

5. As works original, then commentaries, and then theses, over against these, became multiplied,

and so vast as to be beyond the range of a clear conspectus of the subject-matter, necessity for compendia arose. Of such is the *Yatîndra-Mata-Dîpikā*, which purports to be a manual devised in order to present a lucid outline of the Viśishṭâ-'dvaita Philosophy and Religion, based on the voluminous literature extant, most of which the author Śrînivāsa, mentions by name in the Conclusion-Chapter. I have inserted in brackets against these works, the names of these authors.*

6. As handbooks were thus desiderated for original works, English renderings of such seem to be in requisition in these modern days of acute oriental research. The East and West are daily being brought into closer bonds. A memorable epoch of this process has just transpired in King George V of Britain having crowned himself with his august consort Queen Mary, on Indian soil in Dehli. Ṛshi Parāśara, in giving an account of the kings of the future in his Vishṇu-Purāṇa who would hold sway over India, wrote thus:—

'Teshû'tsanneshu punaḥ *Kainkilā*
Yavanā bhūpatayo bhavishyanty
a-mūrdhâ-'bhishiktāḥ. [iv. 24. 55].

The word *Kainkila* has never been noticed as another variant by the learned editor of Wilson's

* Some of these were kindly traced out for me by my friend Prof. M. T. Narasiṁhieṅgār, Bangalūr.

Vishṇu-Purâṇa, Mr. F. Hall. To my mind it sounds very much like (*Ângila*). *Kainkila*-Yavanas then (to us) are the English people. They would rule, he further tells us, *without wearing the crowns* (*a-mûrdhâ-'bhishikta*). This is considered by the Hindus as unorthodox or un-normal. George V. *coronating* himself in India then is an event which restores to the Hindus its own notions and sentiments of what properly constituted sovereigns ought to be (i. e., *mûrdhâ-'bhishikta*). May not the Ṛshi's prophecy point to the necessity of real *crowned* heads establishing themselves in India, instead of *uncrowned* vicegerents being permitted to fulfil royal functions? No literary work written during this Coronation epoch should hence launch out into the world without chronicling this world-event,—an event conspiring to unite East and West in closer bonds of love for co-operative work in future. This is fostered by literary works of the East presented to the West in western garb. My present attempt is one more of this description.*

* 'Our task is to translate ancient knowledge into modern equivalents. We have to clothe the old strength in a new form. The new form *without* that old strength is nothing but a mockery; almost equally foolish is the savage anachronism of an old-time power without fit expression. Spiritually, intellectually, there is no undertaking, but we must attempt it.' [Sister Nivedita *alias* Margaret E. Noble].

Also it is significant to note that as this work is being sent out on its career, the Government of India has resolved to take practical steps to encourage Oriental Learning, judging from the Blue Book just published of the transactions of the Conference of Orientalists held in Simla, last July, under the presidentship of Sir S. Harcourt Butler, C.S.I., C.I.E., Member of Council for Education.

7. Three Editions of the *Yatīndra-Mata-Dīpikā* have come to my knowledge:—

(1) Published by the Vedānta-Vidyā-Vilāsa Press, Madras, 1868, in *Telugu* characters.

(2) Published by the Vidyā-taraṅgiṇī Press, Mysore, 1896, in *Telugu* characters.

(3) Pūna Ānandâ-"śrama Series, No. 50. 1906, with a commentary by Vāsudeva Šāstrin, in *Devanāgarī*. *Variæ lectiones* is almost nil, but a good edition along with English translation seems a future contingency.* The author has divided the work into Ten *Avatāras*, i.e., Incarnations, in allusion to the fact of Vishṇu's (Nārāyaṇa's) Ten Incarnations. Conforming with this sentiment, have I adopted the equivalent term *Advent* to mean Sections or Chapters.

* There are two *Kārikās* (versified works) treating of the same subject-matter (come to my notice), (1) *Vedānta-kārikâ-"vaḷi* by Veṅkaṭârya, (2) *Yatīndra-siddhānta-sangraha* by Šrī-sailâ-"cārya. [*Vidyā-taraṅgiṇī Press, Maisūr.*]

As I stated above, the work, being academic, is rather rigid. I would therefore recommend the reader to begin from the Fourth Advent to the End (*prameya* part), and then turn back to the First Three Advents (*pramāṇa* part). In any case the copious notes supplied will, it is hoped, lead to a clear comprehension of the otherwise intricate windings of the Viśishṭâ-'dvaita Philosophy and Religion.

8. Finally, I have to note that this addition to the Orientalia was finished on the 2nd of February 1912, the auspicious day on which a great festival is held in Melkoṭe Hill (Tiru-Nārāyaṇa-puram), thirty miles north from Maisūr (Mysore), in honour of Śrī Rāmānuja having discovered the Holy Image of Nārāyaṇa overgrown with jungle and ant-hills, under the asterism *Punarvasu* (pollox).* By accident or providence, it is difficult for the small wits of man to divine, Rev. J. N. Farquhar of the Y. M. C. A. Calcutta, came just now for the first time to Maisūr and in his address to the public in the Wesleyan Mission School hall, began with the preliminary that what attracted him to the place was neither woodland nor river-scene, neither Darya-Daulats nor Tippu's Tombs, but that great Rāmānuja who appeared ten centuries ago on this land giving to men a great spiritual

* See (my) *Life of Rāmānuja*. Ch. xxix.

message.* On the day referred to (2nd February.) the Reverend gentleman, true to his announcement, was closeted with me for nearly two hours, in conversation connected with Šrī Rāmānuja, and he incidentally referred to the lack of the ethical conception of God in the Vedānta, but I told him that the key-note of Rāmānuja's teachings was pre-eminently *that.* This was the very point also, as I discovered, he had already put in print in his *Primer of Hinduism*, (p. 42), where he says that 'in the Vedānta Philosophy there is one fatal omission that Brahman is not conceived as holy; we are nowhere told that Brahman is righteousness..........Hinduism remains from first to last crippled, because the idea of God was never moralised.' It is unfortunate Rev. Farquhar committed himself thus too soon; for he would have made quite a contrary statement if he had written his Primer *after* his South Indian tour; for close

* Combining this event with the coronation event and the swelling body of the Orientalia, read what Justice M. G. Ranade prophesied in 1901, viz., 'The hand of God in History is but dimly seen by those who cannot recognize in the contact of European with Eastern thought a higher possibility for the future of both races. Already the morning dawn is upon us and we can see glimpses of the bright future reflected in our ability to know and appreciate each other's strength and excellence. [*Philosophy of Theism.*]

acquaintance with Rāmānuja would have startled him by his exposition of a most ethical and loving as well as sublime and exalted, God as surpasseth all notions of similar character that may be found enshrined in other Scriptures of Earth. Unfortunately such appellations of Deity connoting His highly ethical character, seem to have escaped his the Revd.'s notice, viz., *dharma, satya, puṇya, pāvana, pavitra, pūta, śuchi, śuddha, śiva, hari, kalyāṇa, amala, apahata-pāpmā, heya-pratyanīka, nish-kalanka antaryāmi,** *Bhagavān* † etc. This *ethical* concept is in fact the cardinal, salient, momentous feature of the Vedānta that constitutes Rāmānuja's evangel to mankind.

9. Christianity no doubt derives its conception of God from the Semitic Judaism, but it ought not to forget its *fons et origo* remote in the mists of ages, *viz.*, the Āryan (or Vedic) Brāhmanism. In the light of ethnographic, philologic, geologic and archæologic

---

* This means God, *immanent* in nature and man, meaning thereby the Holy Guide (or *Ghost*, if that word is more endearing), who, as Justice Ranade puts it, 'is the Divine Reality regulating the purposes of law and order, beauty and benevolence, power and wisdom'.

† See the significations of this last term discussed in the pages of JRAS, for 1910, 1911, 1912, one scholar Dr. Schrader firmly holding that it means essentially *holy*.

knowledge, made available by Orientalists in this age of enlightenment and enlarged horizon, neither to gain nor glory does it redound to ignore the world-old traditions common to the Indo-European race. The outlook is now so wide that it is time the narrow bounds of Hebraism to which Christianity tenaciously clings itself, should be overleaped. The East invites all men to unite. Even as George V was crowned in India, the Universal Religion of all humanity is destined to be crowned here.* The *Science of Religions* by Emile Burnouf is a bracing revelation on this theme. Dr. Deussen, even without his reaching as far as Rāmānuja, says 'that there is not in the Bible (this venerable book being not yet quite free from Semitic realism) †; but it is in the

---

* It is here meet to recall Śrī Pārthasārathi Yogi's proposal to Dr. Miller of Madras to call his College, not Christian, but Universal Religious, College; but Dr. Miller could only heave a sigh, and no more.

† See his *Indian Reminiscences*. Max Muller in his *Lectures on the Vedānta* has shown the high ethical standard of the Vedānta, implicated in the doctrine of *karma*, which the Christian Church impugns to the detriment of all ethics, reducing God to the sorry predicament of a capricious, partial and cruel tyrant, violating as such all essentials of ethics. The Vedāntic Deity, on the other hand, Max Muller shows, embraces the deities of any other religion.

Veda'; and that 'the Vedānta in its unfalsified form, is the strongest support of *pure morality.*' Unless God were *ethical*, Vedānta could not as it doth, sermon on *morality*! Vain again were its teachings of the *immanency* of Spirit, did it not mean a life of *holiness* to have to spring from it!! Any other opinion betokens shortness of insight and slenderness of scholarship in South Indian lore. Even if the ethical idea were germinal in the Veda, it receives its complete expression in Rāmānuja.* Even the stage to which

---

Even the cold light of logical Tyndall confessed to P. C. Mozoomdar that 'life came from the East once before, and it must come again.' (1874 A.D.)

* That such a world-wide *Book of Ethics*, the Bhagavad-Gītā should have escaped the notice of such an earnest and sympathetic missionary as Rev. J. N. Farquhar—a fault venial in the bygone centuries, but not in this 20th century—passeth our understanding. Nor will Hinduism in the least countenance such ethics (?) of the Christian Church as *eternal* damnation for petty sin or *eternal* salvation for petty virtue; both determined, indeed, by the infinitesimal life-span of man on earth, and projecting him for the nonce, into eternity for good or worse heedless of the ends of justice! The soul (ego) itself is an ethical entity to Vedānta (not sinful as Christiany insists, though God Himself breathed it!); *a fortiori*, God in Vedānta is essentially, primarily and exaltedly ethical. Unless God were so, He could

the idea developed in Jesus the Christ's days, is still by ten centuries green. It is scientific to conceive the Kosmos as ceaselessly progressive; and therefore evolution need not be imagined as making an exception in the case of Religion and Philosophy. Their progress therefore cannot be arrested at the Near East, Palestine. If the conservative of Christ be combined with the progressive of Rāmānuja, in whom the germinal of the Veda finds its finale, the world is all the more a gainer. The collective reason of all religions so transmitted in history becomes the common heritage of all mankind.

10. As the man of the Near East (Palestine) Jesus the Christ, was found ready to direct construction when northern barbarians pounced upon and destroyed the classical Roman Empire, the sun of Rāmānuja rose on the horizon of the Middle East (India) to direct construction when trans-, as well as cis,-Himālayan influences such as the Persian (Assyrian also it is said), Semitic and Buddhistic, and all their congeners had well-nigh sublimated the classic Vedic Brāhmaṇism. In this constructive work, Rāmānuja had also to contend against absolute monism and ergo consequential non-ethical character liable to be imputed to Godhood, into which Vedism had been volatilized; landing it in nihilism; and he had also

---

not be an object worthy of *Love*; forasmuch as He is characterized as *Ānanda* in the Vedānta.

to establish the Personality of the Godhead as standing in the most intimate relationship to the Ego (soul), for the redemption of which Divinity maketh repeated loving sacrifices: *Ajāyamāno bahudhā vijāyate*, i. e., Incarnations *; and in order to prepare the same Ego for sweet eternal service comporting with Its Will.

11. Rāmānuja also found that men in his days had swerved from the unitarian conception of God, hidden under poetry, mythe or trope in the Archaic Vedas; and it was therefore his evangel to converge on to this unitarian focus the divergent lines of thought which had emerged from the Vedic source, directing them to a conception of Divinity neither polytheistic nor pantheistic,† neither deistic nor theistic, neither monistic nor dualistic, but a happy synthesis of all the essential features that gave these their names, into a monotheistic Unity (=*Bhāgavata Dharma*), philosophic *cum* religious, intellectual *cum* emotional,—a Unity of Godhood, in short, necessarily ethical and sufficient unto salvation.‡ Also in

---

* Cardinal Newman held that the Christian Church borrowed this doctrine from India. God is *Ānanda* = Love (*Ānando-Brahma*), and therefore incarnates to give and evoke Love (*Esha hy evâ-"nandayāti*). Incarnation implies vicarious suffering. Read *Purusha-Sūkta* and the *Tāṇḍya-Mahā-brāhmaṇa.*

† Read Advent IX. on 'God.'

‡ Read Rāmānuja's *Brahma-sūtra-Bhāshya*, *Gadya-traya &c.*

Rāmānuja may already be discovered the latest evolution of theistic inquiry embodied in such works, for instance, as Prof. C. Fraser's Philosophy of Theism, in which the Three Primary Data: Ego (soul); Matter, and God are elaborately considered,—which is no other than Rāmānuja's Three Postulates of Existence, the *Tattva-Traya*, articulately epitomised in the *Yatindra-Mata-Dīpikā*. Ranade writes:—'As a matter of fact, both before Śankarâ-"cārya's time, and after his death, the modified (*Advaita*) system of Rāmānuja had played a great part in Indian Philosophy, and to it may be traced the rise and progress of Vaishṇava Sects throughout India, which sects have attained to a higher and truer conception of Theism than any of the other prevailing systems'. Again he says:—'The three-fold postulates of existence (*cit*, *acit*, *Īśvara* of Rāmānuja) are thus seen to be distinct and yet harmonized together. All attempts to assimilate and reduce them into one absolute existence fail because they are bound to fail. At the same time they are not distinct in the sense of being disjoined parts of a mechanical whole. They are one and yet they are many.' (i. e. Viśishṭâ-"dvaita).

12. Christianity is a happy combination of Semitic and Āryan culture * in the direction of religion: but

* (1) 'Hebraism and Hellenism', in a restricted sense, according to Mathew Arnold. Semitic comprises Islamic, Chaldic, Accadian, Egyptian, Judaic

Rāmānuja later came to unify the Drāviḍian * also including the Bhāgavata *credo*, which is *par excellence*

---

and Christian faiths. Drāviḍian comprises all the Turanian branches. Āryan includes Persic, Medic, Greecian, Roman, Celtic, Teutonic, Slavonic, Christian. All the three, Āryan, Semitic and Turanian thus engirdle the World. Chaldic (Assyrian) is suspected to be Āryan, and Judaism also, when traced through the Essenes and Ebionites. Dr. Deussen is thus justified. [see p: xv. preface.] .

(2) J. M. Kennedy in his *Religions and Philosophies of the East* p: 6, observes thus;—'One cannot but marvel at the impudence and conceit of the Christian missionary who goes to, say India, after a short course of training and straightway proceeds to confute with specially prepared arguments the doctrines of a belief devised by a much superior class of men --a belief indeed to which Christianity itself can easily be traced.'

(3) Revd. Dr. Miller of Madras asked the British Christians to bear in mind that God was at work in India long before any missionary, Catholic or Protestant, set his foot there.

* Drāviḍian includes the two branches Vaishṇava and Śaiva. The Dramida- or Dravida-Bhāshya on the Brahma-Sūtras, referred to both by Śaṅkara and Rāmānuja, seems to be an ancient commentary, by its very name Dramiḍa of Dramiḍā-"cārya. Anterior to Rāmānuja and posterior to Śaṅkara, procrustean

concerned with the closest personality of Divinity. There is thus a Holy Trinity realised in Rāmānuja, which fuses all the world-faiths into a Universal system. The Theosophical Society also, which sits enthroned in India, in *Madras* too, where Rāmānuja's work largely lay,—stript of all its occultism and esotericism—coupled with other Vedāntic movements, may be taken as the most obvious evidence proving the fulfilment of Rāmānuja's work. Rāmānuja's work is like what Bacon wrote:—'All partitions of knowledge should be accepted, rather for lines to mark and distinguish than for sections to divide and separate, so that the continuance and entirety of knowledge be preserved.'

13. Under such auspices, the riches are presented to the world, contained in the Compendium,—the YATĪNDRA-MATA-DĪPIKĀ.

Veda-Gṛham,
Maisūr (Mysore),
South India.
2nd Febry., 1912.

ĀLKOṆDAVILLI
GOVINDÂ-''CĀRYA SVĀMIN,
M.R.A.S, M.R.S.A, ETC.

---

methods seem to have been prevalent; but Rāmānuja gave true proportions by showing how the radical conceptions of God involved in such terms as Śiva, Hiraṇyagarbha, Indra, Agni *etc.*, were all implicated in the comprehensive term Nārāyaṇa. See Advent IX on 'God.'

CORRIGENDA.

PAGE	LINE	FOR	READ
v	20	he is	is
v	24	*astu*	*asti*
viii	17	Karisaila	Karišaila
xi	17	editon	edition
8	12	(the further	(the further).
14	19	Inference,	Inference
14	21	*Sāṁskara*	*Saṁskāra*
15	9	dor-mant	dormant
18	1	perception	perception,
23	22	dlfferences	differences
28	23	—*Sangraha*	—*Saṁgraha*
36	add after line 16		Because antithesis is wanting
36	17-18-19	because...wanting	(because....wanting)
41	25	*Kālâtyayâya......*	*Kālâtyayâpa......*
42	8	*Kratu,*	*Kratu',*
47	21	intended,	intended.
53	20	*parisapkhyā*	*parisaṁkhyā*
53	24	*Jyotish ṭomam*	*Jyotishṭomam*
54	24	or	of
59	23	*Pankaja*	*Paṅkaja*
63	heading	...knowledge	knowledge; Matter

PAGE	LINE	FOR	READ
88	1	Four-*Yugas*	Each Manu has for his time-measure 71 Four-*Yugas*
91	25	*koti*	*koṭi*
110	23	*saṉgamam*	*saṁgamam*
111	14	Udgita	Udgitha
115	26	*Māyāvadins*	*Māyāvādins*
116	3	Bhaskara	Bhāskara
116	25	Šaivâcaryas	Šaivâcāryas
118	21	Soul,	Soul
123	23	*etc*	*ete*
125	20	Jaimini......*ṉoiya*	Jaiminiya...*shaṉo*
126	11	&c.	&c'.
128	1	abide	abides
129	25	*mantrāšrayaš.*	*mantrâ"šrayaš*
130	9	*Sriman*—	*Šriman*—
133	21	delvered	delivered
145	19	cognizer	cognized
151	2	hypostatize	hypostatizes
154	13	(Easternal	(as Eternal
156	5	non-substance	Non-substance
157	1	*Isvara*	*Īśvara*
158	15	aad	and
162	18	(gallnut)	(gallnut),
167	19	Sixteen	Twenty-four

CLORY TO RĀMĀNUJA

YATĪNDRA[1]-MATA-DĪPIKĀ

OR

THE LIGHT OF RĀMĀNUJA'S SCHOOL.

ADVENT[2] I—PERCEPTION (*Pratyaksha*).

INVOCATORY VERSES.

1. Śrī-Veṅkaṭeśam Kari-śaila-nātham
Śrī-Devarājam Ghaṭik-ādri-siṁham
Kṛshṇena sākam Yatirājam īḍe
Svapne ca dṛshṭān mama Deśik-endrān.

2. Yatīśvaram praṇamyā 'ham
Vedānt-āryam Mahā-gurum
Karomi bāla-bodhārtham
Yatīndra-mata-dīpikām.

The Blessed Lord (*Śrīman-Nārāyaṇa*)[3] alone is the Truth (*tattva*), adjectivated by soul

---

[1] The 'King of Yatis' or ascetics = Rāmānuja.

[2] I have adopted 'Advent' for the Saṁskṛt word *Avatāra.*

[3] *Śrī* means Blessed, metaphorically She is *Lakshmī* or the Mediatrix, the Mother. *Nārāyaṇa* is the All-

and non-soul,[4] and secondless. By Love (*Bhakti*) and Resignation (*Prapatti*,) propitiated, He alone is the Means;[5] and He alone is the Goal, adjectivated by the Spiritual Universe. Thus, by means of the texts (or passages) of the Vedānta, do *they* establish—viz., Vyāsa, Bodhāyana, Guhadeva, Bhāruci, Brahmānandi, Dramiḍācārya, Śrī Parāṅkuśa,[6] Nātha,[7] Yāmunamuni,[8] Yatīśvara[9] and others. According to their School, I proclaim, by the grace of Mahācārya (my Guru or Spiritual Preceptor), the

---

God, and metaphorically He is the Father. Thus Śrīman-Nārāyaṇa = The Universe's Mother-Father Principle = God.

[4] The original expression is *Chid-achid-viśishṭa*. *Chit* = conscious entity = Soul; and *Achit* = Non-conscious entity = Non-soul. Nārāyaṇa is thus the Soul-and-Non-soul-bodied-Spirit = God.

[5] That is Means to Salvation or Deliverance from the Material State, and for attaining the Spiritual State.

[6] This is Śaṭhagopa or St. Nammāzhvār [*vide* our *Lives of Saints*].

[7] Or Nāthamuni [*vide* our *Life of Rāmānuja*].

[8] Or Āḷavandār [*vide* Op. cit].

[9] Or Rāmānuja [*vide* Op. cit].

Šārīraka-Paribhāshā,[10] named Yatīndra-mata-Dīpikā (or the Light of Rāmānuja's School),—which follows the Vedānta—for the instruction of students.

All the sum of things are divisible into two Divisions, (1) *Pramāṇa*, Authority, or *Measurer* or Means (of knowledge), and *Prameya* or the *Measured* or Object (or Objective) (of knowledge).

The Means (of knowledge) is only threefold.

The Object (of knowledge) is twofold, *Dravya* or the Thing (or Substance), and *A-dravya* or the Non-Thing (or Non-Substance).

Dravya or Substance is of two kinds, *Jaḍa* or the Non-sentient [11] and *A-jaḍa* or the Sentient [11].

---

[10] *Literally*: Bodied-Technology; or a technology, terminology or phraseology pertaining to the Corporeated. The *Corporeated* is the All-bodied God (Nārāyaṇa) and that treatise which discusses, or discourses on, Him, is also called the *Šārīraka*, or the Philosophy of the Corporeated or The Philosophy and Religion of the Vedas.

[11] *Non-conscient* and *Conscient* would perhaps be more appropriate. Literally *jaḍa* is inert, and *a-jaḍa* is then its opposite: *ert* or non-inert. *Non-intelligent* and *Intelligent*: is another useful pair of terms.

Jaḍa or the Non-sentient is twofold, viz., *Prakṛti* or Matter and *Kāla* or Time.

Prakṛti or Matter is composed of twenty-four (sub-) principles (*tattva*).

Kāla or Time is, by reason of limitation or condition (*upādhi*), threefold.

A-jaḍa or the Sentient is twofold; *Parāk* or outward (objective) and *Pratyak* or Inward (subjective).

Parāk or Outward is also twofold: the *Nitya-vibhūti* or Eternal Estate, and the *Dharma-bhūta-jñāna* or attributive (or adjectival) consciousness or cognition.

Pratyak or Inward is also twofold: *Jīva* or the Individual Soul and *Īśvara* or Ruling (Universal) Soul (God).

Jīva or Individual Soul is threefold: (1) *Baddha* or the Bound, (2) *Mukta* or the Freed, and (3) *Nitya* or the Eternal (or Free).[12]

The *Baddha* or bound soul is also twofold:

---

[12] Cf: Pp. 572ff $\frac{\text{J. R. A. S.}}{\text{A.D. 1910}}$ —*Artha-Pañcaka* or "The Five Truths".

Bubhukshu or Pleasure-desirer,[13] and *Mumukshu* or Freedom-desirer.[14]

The *Bubhukshu* or Pleasure-desirer is twofold: the addicted to *Artha*[15] or wealth, and *Kāma*[15] or gratifications; and the devoted to *Dharma*[15] or Duties.

The devoted to *Dharma* or duties are twofold: the devoted to godlings, and the devoted to Bhagavān[16] (God).

The *Mumukshu* or Freedom-desirer is twofold: the addicted to *Kaivalya* or Isolation,[17] and the devoted to *Moksha* or Salvation.[18]

The *Moksha* or Salvation-seeker is twofold:

---

[13] *Pleasure* here is meant for material enjoyments or sense-delights, either on earth or transmundane spheres such as *Svarga*; or what may be called the material paradise.

[14] *Freedom* here is meant liberation or emancipation from all material associations or pleasures. It means salvation, or bliss in spiritual estate.

[15] *Cf.* Pp: 577 *ff.* $\frac{\text{J. R A. S.}}{\text{A.D. 1910}}$ for details.

[16] See *Op. cit.* Pp: 861 *ff.* (passim).

[17] Soul-bliss or Self-abstraction, See *Op. cit.* Pp: 577 *ff.*

[18] God-bliss or Conscious God-union, See *Op. cit.* Pp: 577 *ff.*

the *Bhakta*[19] or God-lover, and the *Prapanna*[20] or God-resigned.

The *Prapanna* or God-resigned is twofold: the *Ekānti* or the One-pointed, and the *Paramâikānti* or the One-only-pointed.

The *Paramâikānti* is twofold: the *Dṛpta*[21] or The Postulant-Patient, and the *Ārta*[21] or The Postulant-Impatient.

Īśvara or God Supreme is (hypostatically) existent in five modes, viz., (1) *Para* or the Transcendant, (2) *Vyūha* or the Grouped, (3) *Vibhava* or the Incarnational (4) *Antaryāmi* or the In-Ruler, and (5) *Arcā* or the Worshippable.[22]

Para or the Transcendant is Uniform (or the Immutable Spirit-Unit).

Vyūha or the Grouped is fourfold: (1) Vāsudeva, (2) Saṅkarshaṇa, (3) Pradyumna, and (4) Aniruddha. Keśava and others are derivative

---

[19] & [20], See *Op. cit.* Pp: 581*ff.*

[21] See *Op. cit.* Pp. 585*ff.* Supplicant may be used for Postulant and Votary for popular use.

[22] See *Op. cit.* Pp. 576*ff.* Variant terms are used, that Western minds may apprehend the ideas involved in the Saṁskṛt terms.

(*Logal*) groups. The Matsya or the Fish and other Incarnations are innumerable.[33]

Antaryāmi or the In-Ruler dwells in every body.

Arcā or the Worshippable are those unique Images presented to the eyes of all men in such Holy Shrines as Śrīraṅgam.[34]

An examination will now be conducted in order of this specification (or enunciation) above made (of the categories).

Of those, *Pramāṇa* or Means of knowledge is the producer (or maker or giver) of *Pramā* or knowledge. 'Means' is what is to be defined; the definition of it is that 'it is the producer of *Pramā*, knowledge'. *Pramā* is *jñāna* or 'knowledge consonant with experience in its exactitude'. *Pramā* or knowledge is the thing to be defined. The definition is 'that which

---

[33] See *Tattvatraya* of Lokācārya (No. 2, in the list, P. 570. *Op. cit.*,) for an explanation of the functions performed by what may be called the *Logoi* derived from the One Spirit, *Para*. Also read Pp. 82-83 of our *Vade Mecum* of *Vedānta*.

[34] Near Trichinopoly, South India. Raṅga or Nārāyaṇa is here figured as recumbent on the coils

has the quality of knowledge consonant with experience in its exactitude'. Supposing the definition of *Pramā* was simply 'knowledge', the knowledge which sees silver in a pearl-oyster would be a definition overlapping its bounds (*ati-vyāpti*),[25] (or over-pervading its legitimate limits). Hence the definition of *Pramā* takes the form: 'knowledge consonant with experience'. Even then the fault of over-pervasion (*ati-vyāpti*) remains, inasmuch as one in a moment of illusion (or delusion) may mistake the pearl-oyster for silver. Hence (the further) qualificatory clause to the definition: 'in its exactitude (*yathâvasthita*)'.[26] By this expression, *samśaya, anya-*

of Śesha or the Serpent. For symbology see Introd: to our *Lives of Saints*. See *note* 49 *infra*.

[25] *Ati-vyāpti* is one of the three faults to which a definition is exposed. The fault *ati-vyāpti* or *Inclusion* would include things beyond the scope of the definition. The other fault is *a-vyāpti* or *Exclusion* of things which ought to fall within the definition intended. The third fault is *a-sambhava*, or *Non-existence*, or Negation, example: the definition of a sky-flower. See *infra* P.9.

[26] Naturalness, or Naturality would be apt. Another expression which may be employed is reality, or actuality. The whole definition may stand thus as an alternative: 'Knowledge exact to,

thā-jñāna and *viparīta-jñāna* are avoided (which would) otherwise vitiate the definition.

Saṁśaya or Doubt is the apperception of mutually contradicting attributes in a thing (*dharmī*) to be apprehended. For example, the doubt whether a long-looking or erect object is post or person.

Anyathā-jñāna or Wrong Apprehension is the mistaken apperception of one *attribute* for another. For example, the proposition which ascribes the agency in the real agent, soul, as due to illusion. (This is *dharma-viparyāsa*).

Viparīta-jñāna or Reversed Apprehension is the mistaken apperception of one *thing* itself for another. (For example the mistaking of the post itself for the person). (This is *dharmi-viparyāsa*).

A definition (or sign of a thing) has three faults, (1) *a-vyāpti*, (2) *ati-vyāpti* and (3) *a-sambhava*[27]. *A-vyāpti* or non-pervasion is the non-existence of the sign[28] (or definition) in the thing signified[29] (or to be defined). *Ati-vyāpti*

---

or with, practicality'; 'the reality of empirical knowledge' will perhaps better help our readers.

[27] See note 25. [28] *Lakshaṇa*. [29] *Lakshya*.

or over-pervasion is the existence of the sign (or definition) in things other than the things to be signified. *A-sambhava* is the non-existence of the sign (or definition) anywhere. For example the statement (or assertion) that *Jīva* or the Individual Soul is an object of perception by the eye.

As therefore these faults are absent in the definition given of *Pramāṇa* or Means of knowledge, that definition is well established.

(Now in the proposition, *Pramā-karaṇa* = *Pramāṇa*, i.e., the producer of knowledge, is the Means of knowledge, what is meant by *Karaṇa*, producer, maker or effecter?). *Karaṇa* or producer is that which is the best instrument (by which knowledge is obtained). The best instrument is the instrument than which there is none better. Hence it is evident that *Pramāṇa* or the Means of Knowledge is that instrument than which there is none better by which to obtain (that) knowledge.

There is a definition of *Pramāṇa* as that which makes known what is unknown. But those who propose this definition have themselves refuted it. Hence it is not acceptable.

The *Pramāṇas* or the Means of knowledge are three :—(1) *Pratyaksha* or Perception,[30] *Anumāna* or Inference, and *Šabda* or Word.

Of these, Perception is the Means which renders knowledge actually sensible (or made manifest to the senses). 'Manifest to the senses' is (a necessary clause) to show its[31] variety from Inference. *Pramā* or knowledge is to show its character different from what it would be to the vitiated (unsound, defective or diseased) sense.

This Perception is twofold: *Sa-vikalpaka* or collective,[32] and *Nir-vikalpaka* or general.[33] *Nir-vikalpaka* or general, is superficial Knowledge of a thing consisting in its attributes, form *etc.*, obtained at first sight. *Sa-vikalpaka*, general or particular, is thorough Knowledge of a thing consisting in its attributes, form *etc.*, obtained on deep reflexion (or meditation).[34]

---

[30] *I.e.*, Sense-perception, or sensuous perception.

[31] *I.e.*, Perception by senses.

[32] *I.e.*, thorough, in popular language.

[33] *I.e.*, superficial, in popular language.

[34] Thus *Nir-vikalpaka* would be *shallow*, whereas *Sa-vikalpaka* would be *deep*, knowledge.

In both cases, attributes, form *etc.*, are ancillary *sine qua non*; for if these ancillaries (or auxiliaries) were absent, the knowledge (of a thing) is neither present [35] nor known. [36]

The process of perception is thus: (1) the soul's [37] contact with the mind, (2) the mind [38] with the sense, and (3) the sense [39] with the object. [40] The invariable function of the senses is to illuminate the object to be perceived. (For example), the contiguity of the sense, eye *etc.*, with the object, pot *etc.*, causes the ocular knowledge: "This is the pot". Thus also are the tactual and other perceptions. In the perception of a thing, contact is the connexion. In the perception of the form *etc.*, of a thing, (the relation or connection called) *Samavāya* [41] or

---

[35] *An-upalambha* is the scientific term. It means that a thing devoid of attributes, form etc., is beyond recognition or perception.

[36] *An-upapatti*. *Upapatti* is known by conclusive reasoning. Hence *An-upapatti* is not so known; i.e., inconclusive; or what fails to be.

[37] The technical term is *Ātmā*.

[38] The technical term is *Manas*.

[39] The technical term is *Indriya*.

[40] The technical term is *Artha*.

[41] *Nitya-sambandhas; samavāyah*: The invariable or

inherence is inadmissible, for the connection is one of dependence on the thing depended upon.

The perceptions *Nir-vikalpaka* (or general)[42] and *Sa-vikalpaka* (particular)[42] are twofold: *Arvācina* or memorial[43] (*lit.* recent) and *Anarvācina* or non-memorial[44] (=ancient or primal *lit.* remote). The memorial again is twofold: sense-helped and sense-unhelped.

The sense-unhelped is twofold: *Svayaṁsiddha* or self-ascertained, and *Divya* or divine. Self-ascertained is what is engendered by Yoga or deep meditation. Divine is what is caused by Bhagavān's (God's) Grace.

The non-memorial is sense-unhelped, or the knowledge possessed by the *Nityas*[45] or the Eternals and the *Muktas*[45] or the Emancipated.

---

inseparable relation of a thing or substance with its attributes or *vice versa*.

[42] Alternative terms used for better elucidating the ideas.

[43] *I.e.*, Caused or Mediate, or sense-vehicular, subject to time and space.

[44] *I.e.* Uncaused or Immediate, i.e., intuitional, not subject to time and space.

[45] See *Artha-Pañcaka*. Pp. 573 *ff*. $\frac{\text{J. R. A. S.}}{\text{1910 A.D.}}$

This non-memorial (perception) is passingly referred to.

Thus *Pratyaksha* or Sense-Perception is that which generates Sākshātkāra, or knowledge, sense-evident.

But an objection may be put forward thus:—*Pramā* or knowledge has been defined to be knowledge as is actually consonant (or consistent) with experience. This condition is also found present in *Smṛti* or memory; hence memory or recollection must also be counted as a Means of knowledge. How then are such Means (*pramāṇas*) stated to be only Three?[46]"

To this objection it is said: Even if memory be admited as a Means,it is dependent on *Saṁskāra,*[47] or residua left of previous experiences, and these residua are dependent on (sense-) perception. Hence memory is included (or

---

[46] *I.e.*, Perception, Inference, or Inductive Reasoning, and Word or Revelation.

[47] *Bhāshā-pāricchada* says: "*Sāṁskāra*, called thinking (*bhāvanā*), resides in sentient beings; and is imperceptible to the senses. Certainty, devoid of inattention in its constituent, is its cause. It is also described to be the cause of memory and recognition. See also p. 95, Dr. Morell's Mental Philosophy.

involved) in perception, and there is no need to constitute it into a distinct Means or Authority.

Hence the Means (or Authorities or Instruments of knowledge) become determined as Three (only.)

Memory or Recollection is Knowledge derived from the residua or impressions left of a previous (or past) experience. The excitants (that rouse the dormant residua into remembrance) are as per verse:

Sadṛśâ'dṛshṭa-cintā'dyaiḥ
Smṛti-bījasya bādhakāḥ.[48]

Sometimes the excitant is the sight of something similar (previously sensed); sometimes an unseen (or unexpected) fate (*adṛshṭa*); sometimes deep musing. Similarity is thus (exemplified): (1) If two (individuals) Devadatta and Yajñadatta had once been seen together, the sight of Devadatta excites the remembrance of Yajñadatta. (2) The second is the unexpected (i. e., unconscious cerebration) leaping into

[48] The three causes that excite or stimulate recollection are exemplified *infra*. *Lit*: the causes that excite the seed of memory into development or unfoldment, which is remembrance or recollection.

memory, of what has previously been experienced (sensed), such as the Holy Place Śrīraṅgam.[49] (3) The Third is the calling into memory (conscious cerebration) such as the bewitching divine Image of Veṅkaṭeśa [50] (before sensed). What is well experienced engenders constant remembrance. Forgetfulness is caused by much time elapsing (after the prior experience) or by sickness *etc.*, which weaken the residua (*Saṁskāras*).[51] As remembrance (*Smṛti*) is (thus) included in Perception or Sense-evidence,

[49] This is the Holy Shrine near Trichinopoly, Madras Presidency. The traditions say that the Holy Image therein came from *Kshīrābdhi* or Milky Ocean, to Ikshvāku of the Solar Race and bestowed by Śrī-Rāma on Vibīshaṇa, and installed in Śrīraṅgam. For Symbology, see our *Lives of Saints* and *note* 24 *supra*.

[50] Or Śrīnivāsa, the Holy Image on the Hill Tirupati (or Tirumalai), North Arcot District, Madras Presidency. For traditions see *Venkaṭā'cala-Māhātmya*. These are the *Arcā* Forms, *vide* Pp. 576*ff*. *Artha-Pañcaka*, J. R. A. S. / 1910 A.D. In this connection, read: *Ṛg-Veda* X. 155-1: *Arāyi kāṇe Vikaṭe girim gaccha sadânve Śirim-biṭhasya satvabhis tebhish ṭvā cātayāmasi*"

[51] Or render the impressions faded.

recollection (*Pratyabhijñā*) also is included therein such as: 'this Devadatta is that'.

Abhāva or non-existence[52] is also in our School included in Perception inasmuch as non-existence (of a thing) implies (its) existence (at some other place or time), (thus illustrated):—The non-existence[52] of the pot implies clay—(its, i.e. pot's) pre-existence. The destruction[53] of the pot implies potsherds.

Ūhā or Conjecture is the probability: that a certain person, a certain thing, might *happen* to be.

Saṁśaya or Doubt is the uncertainty: as to what sign (name) (*e.g.*) a tree, seen, is known by.

These also (Ūhā and Saṁśaya) are included in Perception.

Also genius (or extraordinary illumination or inspiration) discovered in blessed or holy, persons (such as sages, seers, saints, and prophets) can be classed under Perception.

---

[52] Or absence or non-being or negation.

[53] Or disappearance.

(But there may be erroneous *etc.*, perception, *Bhrama* ?). Even Erroneous Perception is of the real, for:—

'The School of the Vedāntins, holds all knowledge (or all cognition) to be of the real'.[54] For, to the rejection of *A-khyāti* or 'Non-cognition'-,[55] *Ātma-khyāti* or 'self-cognition'-,[56] *Anirvacanīya-khyāti* or 'inexplicable cognition-,'[57] *Anyathā-khyāti* or 'reversed (or perverted) cognition,-'[58] Schools, the School of *Sat-khyāti* or 'right cognition'[59] is

---

[54] The full verse occurs in *Śrī-Bhāshya* thus:

Yathārtham sarva-vijñānam
Iti veda-vidām matam
Śruti-smṛtibhyas sarvasya
Sarvâtmatva-pratītitaḥ. [I: 1. 1. *Atha* etc.].

[55] The attribute of one thing appearing as that of another (*Mīmāṁsakas*).

[56] The self appearing as a thing (*Yogācāra*-Bauddhas).

[57] Appearing neither real nor unreal—hence inexplicable (*Advaitins*).

[58] The form of a thing assumiug another form (*Naiyāyikas*).

[59] The real view or the realistic view that the thing is what it really is (*Viśishṭādvaitins*).

accepted[60]. *Sat-khyāti* or right cognition is the reality of the object of perception (or object of consciousness).

What then is to be erroneous or illusory (in the Perception)? Illusoriness (*Bhrama*) is the absence (*Bādha*) or hindrance to any action arising on a correct apprehension of a thing. We shall discuss it. Thus:—

By virtue of the quintuplicatory combination (or process) of the elements (*Bhūtas*),[61] all the elements are present in all the (compounds), such as Earth[61] *etc.* Hence silver must be present in the pearl-oyster, causing realness (or reality) of the cognition thereof. But when a pearl-oyster is apprehended as such, it is so because the silver-portion is very minute (and eludes notice). In this consists the illusoriness (*Bhrama*) of the cognition. The illusion dis-

[60] There is one more view, the *Asat-khāyati* or unreal view (*Mādhyamika*-Bauddhas).

[61] Called *Bhūtas*, because *effected* from the previous simple substances. The compounded or admixed substances are called *elements*. They are Five: (1) *Ākāśa* (ether), (2) *Vāyu* (air), (3) *Agni* (fire), (4) *Āpas* (water), (5) *Pṛthvī* (earth).

appears because of the major portion (of the oyster) being shell.

The dream-cognition (or consciousness) is also real. For from the Śruti,[62] we learn (or know) that the Supreme Lord (*Parama-Purusha*) creates carriages[63] *etc.*, of temporary duration, proportioned to the (merits of the) several persons who have to experience (the same in dreams).

When a (white) conch-shell is seen as yellow and so forth, (the explanation is that) the bilious[64] rays proceeding from the eye unite with the conch-shell etc., and the yellow of the bile[64] (in the eye) overpowering the white of the shell, is not cognized. Hence a yellow shell is

---

[62] 'What is heard,' *lit.* = the Holy Word, Scriptures or Revelations.

[63] Referring to the passage: "*Na tatra rathā, na ratha-yogā, na panthāno bhavanty atha rathān ratha-yogān pathas sṛjate*". [Brihad-āraṇyakopanishat, VI. 3. 10].

[64] Owing to certain diseases like jaundice, the eye becomes color-blind, and sees all white things as yellow. This is called *pitta* in Saṁskṛt supposed to be caused by bile or biliousness.

visualised like a shell gold-plated (or gold-gilt). The yellowness, because it is subtle and issues from the eye, is perceivable by that eye (alone).

The crystal-stone placed in juxtaposition to a China-rose is perceived as red. This perception is also of the real.

As observed already, by reason of the quintuplication of elements, the cognition of water in the mirage is also valid.

The process, (known as) the elemental quintuplication (*Pañci-Karaṇa*) will be described further on.

Mistaking the direction (*Dig-bhrama*) is also of the same character, for one direction (or point of the compass) is involved in another; for all such distinctions of direction cannot be except by division; else no such thing as direction (*Dik*) is admissible.[65]

In the circle described by a fire-brand etc., the cognition (as circle instead of point) arises from the rapidity of the revolution which sets

---

[65] *I.e.*, As when a person thinks the West to be where the East is.

the point at every part of the circle. That is also of the real.[66]

The reflexion of one's face in the mirror *etc.*,[67] is also of a fact; for the eye-rays are intercepted by the mirror, and the eye sees along with the mirror *etc.*,[67] its own face *etc.*, Even in this case the process is so rapid as to prevent the perception of all that may intervene between (the eye and the mirror).

In such cases as the cognition of a double moon (instead of one) it is caused through the pressure of the finger (on the eye), or owing to eye-affections *(timira)* etc., when the visual rays stream in different directions. The apparatus being thus duplicated, independent of each other, causes the double-moon vision.[68] The

---

[66] This is the fiery wheel caused by a brand swung rapidly round, so rapidly that the intervals between any two points are not apprehended by the eye.

[67] *Etc.*, stands for similar reflecting surfaces.

[68] The phenomenon of refraction is known, and where refraction is further influenced by obliquity of vision by any of the aforesaid causes, objects become duplicated at different foci so created.

duplication of the apparatus being a fact, the double-moon cognition takes place.

Hence all cognitions are of the real, and their contents (are provided by) concrete (i.e. attributived) objects; for an attribute-less (or quality-less) object is never cognizable. [69]

Perception then as enunciated (above), apprehends difference alone. When difference (*Bheda*) is posited, it (always) implies a counter-entity, but never [70] (when viewed) as in itself. Hence the two faults are absent, viz., *An-avasthā* or infinite regress, and *Anyo'nyâ"śraya* or mutual

---

[69] Such a thing therefore as *abstract* consciousness, in other words cognition of object *without* any attribute, is a non-entity to the *Viśishṭādvaita* philosophers.

[70] This would appear to mean that when a jar is cognised, it is so cognised as different from a counter-entity which is not a jar, but say a club. Difference thereof is of different objects, not in the same object itself, i.e., difference, inherent. In other words, every transaction necessarily involves differences. and implies counter-entities, which are inadmissible in the province of essentiality. The jarness of a jar is its essentiality. Its distinction from a rod is its difference.

dependence.[71] *An-avasthā* is the (fault of) demanding further and further.[72] *Anyo'nyâ"śraya* is (the fault of) mutual dependence[73].

It may be asked why: 'thou art the tenth',[74] should not also be classed under Perception? We say 'no', for though 'Thou' is certainly a sensuous fact *(Pratyaksha)*, 'the *tenth* thou art' is a cognition which has arisen from (an uttered) sentence. But if it be contended that: 'thou art the tenth' ought to fall under Sensuous Perception, then (by parity of reasoning): 'thou

---

[71] Known as the circular argument, or begging the question (*petitio principii*).

[72] *I.e.*, Absence of finality.

[73] *I.e.*, To prove a cause, effect is needed. To prove an effect, cause is needed. A mutual necessitation.

[74] The illustration here is by a story. Ten men crossed a stream. They wished to be assured that all the ten had arrived safe. One amongst them counted the others from one to nine, but forgot himself. Every one did the same but the result was no better, and they began to cry, one and all, for the tenth man as lost! A wise man now came, and learning the cause of their grief, placed them in a row, and counting from one to nine, declared to their joy the tenth man as '*Thou* art the tenth'.

art good ' must also become (or be treated) as a case of Perception. But if that be insisted (or admitted), then it becomes an 'unwarrantable stretch of a principle' (*Ati-prasaṅga*).[75] Hence cognition (or knowledge) derived from such passages as: "That Thou art", is not Perceptive[76].

From all this the position created by (or predications fancied by) mistaken men (*ku-dṛshṭ-ayaḥ*), *viz.*, '*Pramāṇa* or Means is that which engenders perception (*Pratyaksha*) or knowledge;—knowledge so meant is none other than Intelligence;[77]—Intelligence (*Chaitanya*) is three-fold: 1* *Antaḥkaraṇâ-'vacchinna* or that which is conditioned by the Inner Instrument, 2* *Vṛtty-avacchinna* or that which is conditioned by Act (or state), 3* *Vishayâ-'vacchinna* or that which is

[75] Cp. with *Ati-vyāpti* or over-pervasion of a given definition, *vide* note 25.

[76] That is, it is *Anumāna* or Inferentially known, not (sense-) Perceptively. 'That thou art' is a passage from the Chhāndogya-Upanishat [VI. 8. 7] *That* = Brahman or Paramâtman, *thou* = Soul or Jivâtman. The sentence literally means: 'God thou art'.

[77] *I.e.*, Spirit or God considered as the Abstract,—quality-less.

conditioned by object ;—When all the three combine into one, that is actual realisation (*Sākshātkāra*) (*i. e.*, *pratyaksha* or real knowledge) ;—and that realisation is of the objectless (or a thing devoid of attributes), and of the non-dual (or non-difference)' is refuted[78].

The School of the Naiyāyikās[79] also, viz., '*Nir-vikalpaka* or general (unqualified) knowledge is cognition which but apprehends the *mere* thing as dissociated from all such (attributes) as *Jāti* or class (or genus) etc.,' is also refuted. But it may be asked how such a School as that

---

[78] *Intelligence* enwrapped becomes the *knower* (1).* This is soul. Wrapped by the mediate apparatus, it becomes the *Instrument of Knowledge* (2)*. This is mind and the senses. Wrapped again it becomes the *known* (3)*. This is object. Thus the Abstract or Essence or the Substrate, the 'thing in itself', the Brahman, which is of the nature of Intelligence, is the *Subjective*. This by limitation becomes the *Subject* or Soul; by further limitation becomes the *Instrument* or Mind, etc., and by yet another limitation, the *Objective*. All the three must merge into one, and that is realisation or ultimate knowledge realised, which is no other than perception itself (*pratyaksha*). This is the *Advaita* position.

of Gautama[79] is so lightly refutable when there exist such (authoritative) texts as:—

'Kāṇāda[80] and Pāṇinīya[81] are helpful to all sciences (*Šāstra*)'?

To this it is replied: no School is *in toto* refuted. Whatever stands to reason is accepted, like water in a reservoir constructed by others, but surely never the mire in it.

Hence we do not accept such postulations as:

The Causation by atoms,—

The Human origin of the *Vedas* (Revelations),—

The Inferential Proof for God-hood (*Īšvara*),—

The Infiniteness of Soul (-essence) (Jīva),—

The adoption as categories (*Padārtha*):—

(1) *Sāmānya* or universality (what constitutes

---

[79] The School of Gautama or Gotama,—the Indian School of Logic.

[80] Kaṇāda is the Expounder of a System of Categories known as the *Vaišeshika*, a variety of *Nyāya*. The distinguishing feature of this philosophy is the theory of atoms *(Aṇus)*. *Kaṇa* means atom.

[81] *I.e.*, The Aphorisms of Pāṇini on Grammar, or properly The Science of Language.

[80] + [81] The original is:—*Kāṇādam Pāṇinīyañca sarva-Šāstropakārakam.*

a genus), (2) *Viśesha* or Particularity (what constitutes a species or the Individual), (3) *Samavāya* or Inhesion (or Inherence),—

The constituting *Upamāna* or comparison into a (distinct) Means (of knowledge—*Pramāṇa*),—

The treatment as attributes (or qualities): (1) Number (*Saṅkhyā*), (2) Extension or Quantity or (*Parimāṇa*), (3) Severalty (*Pṛthaktva*), (4) Priority or Anteriority (*Paratva*), (5) Posteriority (*Aparatva*), (6) Solidity (*Gurutva*), (7) Viscidity or Fluidity (*Dravatva*), *etc.*,—

The assumption that direction (*Dik*) is a substance (*dravya*),—and so forth.*

That we accept what is not opposed to reason is (hence) not objectionable.

Thus ends Advent I,
The Treatment of Perception (*Pratyaksha*)
in the
"Light of the School of Rāmānujā"

---

* These matters are further noticed in the following Advents (or Chapters). Also read such works as *Tarka-Saṁgraha*, *Nyāya-bodhinī*, *Tarka-Sangraha-Dīpikā*, *Prakāśikā*, *Ṭippaṇī*, *Bhāshā-Pariccheda* &c.

ADVENT II—INFERENCE (*Anumāna*).

Now, *Anumāna* or Inference will be expounded:

That knowledge (*Pramiti*) is Inferential knowledge (*Anumiti*), which is the particular knowledge of the pervading (*Vyāpaka*),[82] obtained from the consideration of the pervadedness of the pervaded (*Vyāpaka*)[82]. The Instrument or Means by which such knowledge is obtained is Inference (*Anumāna*). (Illustration): Knowing that smoke is pervaded by fire, the knowledge of the pervading is obtained, *i.e.*, fire.

The Pervaded (*Vyāpya*) is ruled by limitedness of space and time. The Pervading (*Vyāpaka*) has the Characteristic (*vṛtti*) of

[82] *Vyāpya* and *Vyāpaka* are technical terms of Hindu Noëtics. In the sentence: 'smoke is pervaded by fire', it means that the one is invariably found with the other. *Vyāpti* would be the invariable or universal concomitance of two things; or the inseparable connection of the one with the other, *sine quâ non*. In the illustration, smoke is the *Pervaded*,

non-limited space and time.[83] The Pervaded is even in inseparable conjunction (with the Pervading). The Pervading is the correlate (or Co-ordinate to the Pervaded). The invariable fixed relation subsisting between the two is Pervasion (*Vyāpti*). This Pervasion, stated as: 'Where there is smoke, there is fire' is admitted, from frequent (or repeated) observation.[84]

Pervasion is twofold: Positive (*Anvaya*) and Negative (*Vyatireka*). Where by an Inferrant (*Sādhana*) the Inferred (*Sādhya*) is attempted, that Pervasion is called Positive, for example: 'Whatever is smoky is fiery'[85], where, by the denial of the Inferred (*Sādhya*), the denial of

---

fire the *Pervading*, element. *Vyāpti* may perhaps be rendered by *co-concurrence* of two or more facts.

[83] This means that fire is a more universal term than smoke, for there may be fire where there is no smoke, but where there is smoke there is fire. Cp. this with the *major* term and *middle* term of logic, the *minor* term being the place where fire is found (say mountain). *Vyāpya* is thus the Particular, and *Vyāpaka* the Universal.

[84] That is to say, the general statement is by induction from several particular instances.

[85] That is, wherever smoke is observed, there is fire (as in a hill)—(by *Agreements*, in other words).

the Inferrant (*Sādhana*) is attempted, that Pervasion (*Vyāpti*) is Negative, for example: 'What is non-fiery is non-smoky'.[86] Both these kinds of Pervasion is affected or circumscribed by conditions (*Upādhi*). Condition (*Upādhi*) means where the Inferred (*Sādhya*) pervades, the Inferrant (*Sādhana*) does not pervade. For example, where, by fire, smoke is intended to be inferred, the condition (required) is conjunction with moist firewood;* or where brownness is intended to be inferred by being the son (or sonness) of Maitrī, the condition is the circumstance of such birth (caused) by (eating) cooked greens.[87]

---

[86] That is, when the hill has no fire in it, it has no smoke. (by *Differences*, in other words).

* Such a condition is absent in a heated iron ball. *Upādhi*, in other words is that which always co-exists with the *major* term, and not always so with the *middle* term. See note on '*Upādhi*' p. 275. Appendix to Mādhavacārya's *Sarva-Darśana-Saṁgrahā* [by E. B. Cowell &c., Trubner & Co., London].

[87] That is: where the cause of brownness of a son is intended to be inferred because of his birth from his mother Maitrī, a circumscribing condition for

Condition or Limitation (*Upādhi*) is twofold: Settled (*Niścita*) and Doubted (*Śaṅkita*).

The *Settled* is thus:—

(*Assertion*) 'The disputed [89] service [88] is woeful, (= *Conclusion*)

(*Reason*) Because it partakes of servitude,

(*Instance*) Like service to a king.'

In this (syllogism), the condition *Upādhi*) (of serving a king, which is distasteful to the servitor) is provided by (one's) sin being the determinant. But this does not exist in the service to God. This therefore is called the *Settled* condition.[88]

The *Doubted* is thus:—

(*Assertion*) 'The disputed [89] soul, after the term of this body, attains Release (*Mukti*) (= *Conclusion*).

---

such a fact may suggest the cause to be due to his eating of green vegetables. The inference of a cause from an effect is thus affected by some condition.

[88] That is, that soul is to serve God is a condition of a *settled* nature.

[89] Disputed means a disputed point,—a questioned assertion. That is, God-service may, or not, be a fact. Such an entity as soul may, or not, exist. A moot-point.

(*Reason*) Because, meditation is ripe,
(*Instance*) Like Šuka.[90]

In this (syllogism), the condition (required) is the surceasal of all actions or works (*Karma*). As it is doubtful whether such a condition exists or no in a problematical soul,—meditation-ripe—that condition is called the *doubted*.

Hence, where a connection (or relation) exists unaffected by condition (*Nir-upādhika*), that which is so connected is the Pervaded (*Vyāpya*).

Pervaded (*Vyāpya*), Means or Instrument (*Sādhana*), Sign (*Liṅga*), are not of different import[91]. *This has two forms, which are limbs (i.e., factors or elements) to Inferential knowledge (*Anumiti*):—(1) Pervasion (*Vyāpti*),[92] and

---

[90] The great sage, the son of Vyāsa.

[91] *I.e.*, they are synonymous terms.

[92] The definition of *Vyāpti* is:—'*Yatra dhūmas tatrâ 'gnir iti sāhacarya-niyamo VYĀPTIḤ*' i.e, where invariable attendedness or con-comitance holds, such as 'where smoke is, there is fire'. *Vyāpti* or Pervasion (a technical term) thus means the indiscerptible co-existent relation between two things.

(2) Subject-attributiveness [93] (*Paksha-dharmatā*)[94].

It has also five forms. They are :—

(1) The being attributive to subject (*Paksha-dharmatā*),

(2) The presence in right place (*Sa-Paksha-tva*),

(3) The absence from wrong place (*Vi-paksha-vyāvṛtti*),

(4) Not annulled by, or inexceptionable (*A-bādhita-vishayatva*),

(5) Absence of equal antithesis (*A-sat-prati-paksha*).

Paksha (Subject) is the substance (*Dharmi*) in which the inferrable attribute (*Dharma*)

---

[93] Subject = *terminus minor* (smoking mountain),
Predicate = *terminus major* (smokiness),
Middle term = *terminus medius* (fieriness).
Smoke found in the mountain, and smoke always accompanying fire, are thus the two *signs* or reasons by which to infer fire in the mountain.

[94] The definition of *Paksha-dharmatā* is.—'*Vyāpyasya parvatâdi-vṛttitvam*', i.e., the existence of the Pervaded in mountain *etc.*, such as, 'the smoke seen is found to exist in the mountain'.

exists; such as the mountain etc., in which the fieriness (Predicate) is to be established.

Sa-paksha (Right Subject or Place) is the similarity to that where an attribute is to be established; such as the kitchen-hearth etc.

Vi-paksha (Wrong Subject or Place) is the dissimilarity to where an attribute is to be established; such as the lake etc.

Bādhita-vishayatva (annulled thing) is the absence of what is to be surely established in the subject by strong reasons (to the contrary); such as: 'the lake is fiery'. 'Not so annulled' is *A-bādhita-vishayatva*.

A-sat-pratipakshatva [98] is the non-annulment by an equally strong reason.

The *Vyāpya* (or Inferential instrument) so described is two-fold: (1) *Anvaya-vyatireki*

---

[98] A negative instance, or an instance on the opposite side, or that in which the *Sādhya* the Inferred or the *terminus major* (predicate, i.e., fieriness) is not found; such as the negation of fieriness in a lake (of water), as its assertion can be made in a hearth. *Et seq.*

Sat-pratipaksha means that where a reason exists to disprove what is to be proved:—*Yasya sādhyābhāva-sādhakam hetv-antaram vidyate sa sat-pratipakshaḥ.*

(Present-Absent), (2) *Kevalâ-'nvayi* (Present only).

The aforesaid five-formed Pervasion (i.e., *Vyāpti* or Instrument) is of the Present-Absent. Thus:—

Anvayi (Present):

'The mountain is fiery,
Because it is smoky,
For whatever is smoky is fiery,
As the kitchen-hearth.

Vyati-reki (Absent):

Whatever is non-fiery is non-smoky,
Like the lake.'

Vyati-reki + Anvayi. — Absent + Present

The same without the *Vipaksha* (antithesis) is the *Kevalānvayi* (Present only, form). Thus:—

Kevalân-vayi (Present only):

'Brahman is Word-[26] expressible,
Because It is a thing,
Like the jar.'

Hence the *Kevalâ-'nvayi* is four-formed, because the fifth, the antithesis (*Vipaksha*) is wanting.

A *Kevala-vyatireki* (Absent only) form, is inconceivable inasmuch as *Sādhya* (predicate

[26] *I.e.*, Revelational or Scriptural Word. It means, Scriptures alone can speak of God. This is in contrast to Natural Theism.

or major term) is nowhere. Hence a purely *Vyatireki* is excluded (or inadmissible).

That either the *Kevalâ-'nvayi* or the *Anvaya-vyatireki* concerns only the supersensuous objects is (thus) repudiated.*

The aforesaid *Anumāna* (Inference), say some, is divisible into two kinds: (1) *Svārtha* or Self-benefit, (2) *Parārtha* or Others' benefit. Others (opine): it is of the 'self' character alone, inasmuch as all inferences are ensuant on the power of one's own reflection, and hence useful for one's own procedure.

The syllogism that establishes an Inference consists of five members:

1. *Pratijñā*—Assertion,
2. *Hetu*—Reason,
3. *Udāharaṇa*—Instance,
4. *Upanaya*—Application (or Deduction),

*That is, the opinion that inferential 'Means' establishes only objects beyond the cognition of the senses, is not admitted. This position is that of the Natural Theologians as contrasted with the Orthodox or Scriptural Theologians. The *Naiyāyikas* think that God can be proved by Inference; but the Vedāntins affirm that such a proof is unstable; whereas proof by Scriptures (Word) is unshakable.

5. *Nigamana*—Conclusion.[97]

In this, *Pratijñā* or Assertion is the sentence indicating the *Paksha* (Subject), thus :—

'The mountain is fiery'.

Hetu or Reason indicates the *Liṅga* (Sign), thus :—

'Because it is smoky'.

Udāharaṇa or Instance is indicating an example where concomitance or co-existence (*Vyāpti*) obtains, and this is twofold; *Anvaya* or Affirmation, and *Vyatireka* or Negation, thus :—

'Whatever is smoky is fiery' is a case of Affirmative Instance.

'Whatever is non-fiery is non-smoky' is a case of Negative Instance.

Upanaya or Application is the sentence which refers the Reason to the subject by a

---

[97] The equivalent *Vaiśeshika* synonyms are:

1. *Pratijñā.*
2. *Apadeśa, Liṅga, Pramāṇa, Kāraṇa.*
3. *Nidarśana.*
4. *Anusandhāna.*
5. *Pratyāmnāya.*

consideration of the Instance. This also is two-fold: Affirmative and Negative; thus:—

'The mountain is smoky,' is of the Affirmative.

'The mountain is not non-smoky' is of the Negative.

Nigamana or Conclusion is the sentence, which conclusively locates what is to be Inferred (*Sādhya*) in the Subject (*Paksha*), by means of the Reason (*Hetu*). This is also twofold, thus:—

(1) 'Therefore the mountain is fiery',

(2) 'Therefore the mountain is non-fiery.'

This five-membered syllogism is of the School of the *Naiyāyika*s or the Logicians.

The *Mīmāṁsakas*[98] uphold a three-membered syllogism, viz., Assertion (*Pratijñā*), Reason (*Hetu*), and Example or Instance (*Udāharaṇa*).

The *Saugatas*[99] hold to a two-membered syllogism, viz., Example (*Udāharaṇa*) and Application (*Upanaya*).

---

[98] The *Vaidikas* of the two Schools *Pūrva* and *Uttara*; or the *Vedāntins*, as may both of them be styled.

[99] The School of the Buddhists divided into *Sautrāntika*, *Vaibhāshika*, *Yogâcāra*, and *Mādhyamika*.

For some it may be five members; for some three, and two for some, but for us there is no restriction. By Example and Application alone, Pervasion (*Vyāpyatva*) and Location (*Paksha-dharmatā*) are established, and Inference is possible from this much alone. That amplifications and abridgements may (severally) suit the (different) dispositions of minds, lowly, middling or lofty, place *us* under no restrictions whatever (as to number).

Thus a well-reasoned five-membered syllogism provides the proof for the fire (in the mountain). 'Well-reasoned' is (advisedly) used in order to guard against an inferential knowledge of fire being attainable by a smoke-resembling volume of dust.

There are specious arguments seemingly valid, called: *Hetv-ābhāsas.*[100] They are:—

1. *Asiddha* (Impossible),

2. *Viruddha* (Reverse),

3. *An-aikāntika* (or *Sa-vyabhicāra*) (Superfluous),

---

[100] *I. e.*, Paralogisms and Sophisms, or Fallacies.

4. *Prakaraṇa-sama* (or *Sat-prati-paksha*) (equi-loquent).

5. *Kālātyayā'padishṭa** (or *Bādhitā*) (Mis-timed).

Of these, *Asiddha* or Impossible is three-fold:—

(1) *Svarūpâ'siddha* or Natural Impossibility,

(2) *Āśrayâ'siddha* or Local Impossibility, and

(3) *Vyāpyatvâ'siddha* or Pervasive Impossibility.

(1) Natural Impossibility is thus (illustrated):—

'The *Jīva* (soul) is eternal,
Because it is visible,
Like the jar.'

(2) Local Impossibility thus:—

'The sky-lotus is fragrant,
For it is of the lotus (species),
Like the pond-lotus.'

Sky-lotus is the *locus* and this is *non-ens*.

(3) Pervasive Impossibility is of two kinds: The one is that where the Means for pervasion is absent, the other where a condition (*Upādhi*)

---

* Also called *Kālātīta* [*vide* Gotama-Sūtras, 50]; '*Kālâtyayâpadishṭaḥ kālātītaḥ*.'

is present. The First is thus :—'Whatever is is momentary'. In this the Means whereby to establish an induction between the 'is' ness and momentariness is absent. The Second is thus :—

'The *Agni-shomiya*[101]'-immolation determines demerit,

For it is of the killing (kind),

Like killing, out of the pale of *Kratu*.'[101]

Here the conditioning comes from the prohibitioning.

Hence the reason of killing is conditioned.

2. The *Viruddha* or reverse-fallacy is that in which the reason is vitiated by the reverse. Thus.—

'Matter (*Prakṛti*) is eternal,
Because it is effected,
Like time.'

Here the reason of 'effected' is pervaded by the negation of the Inferrable.[102]

---

[101] A sacrifice (Vedic) prescribed to the Deities Agni and Soma.

[102] Here what is intended to be proved is the eternality of matter; but in the reason given, a non-eternal element (*viz.*, effectedness) occurs. Hence what is to be proved is negated.

3. The *Anaikāntika* is *Savyabhicāra* or Superfluous:—

This is twofold: (1) *Sādhāraṇa* or Ordinary, (2) *Asādhāraṇa* or Extraordinary. The 'Ordinary' is of the *Paksha*[103] (Subject), *Sa-paksha*[104] (Co-Subject). *Vi-paksha*[105] (Ex-Subject). Thus:—

'Sound is eternal,
Because it is 'object'[106]
Like time.'

The 'Extraordinary' is what is absent from (or non-existent in) *Sa-paksha* (Co-Subject), and *Vi-paksha* (Ex-Subject). Thus:—

'The Earth is eternal
Because it is odorous.'

4. *Prakaraṇa-sama*[107] or Equi-loquent is that where a reason exists which proves (or infers) the negative of that which is to be proved:

---

[103] *I.e.*, the *terminus minor*,—the mountain.

[104] The kitchen-hearth.

[105] The lake.

[106] 'Object' is to translate *Prameya* or that which is cognised by a *Pramāṇa* or Means of Knowledge.

[107] *I.e.*, Which tells equally on both sides.

'God is eternal,
For He is devoid of non-eternality,
God is not eternal,
For He is devoid of eternality.'

This is the same as *Sat-prati-paksha*.[108]

5. *Kālātyayāpadishṭa*[109] or Mis-timed is thus:

'Fire is non-warm,
For it is a substance,
Like water.'

But as fire is actually associated with warmth, the argument is debarred.

Having thus expounded Inference (*Anumāna*,) the others Comparison (*Upamāna*) etc.,[110] are included in Inference. For example, Comparison is said to arise thus:—One, remembering the meaning of an analogous sentence, sees a form

---

[108] '*Yasya bādhyâbhāva-sādhakam hetv-antaram asat-pratipakshaḥ*' [Tarka-Saṁgraha. II].

[109] See mark * p. 41, *lit*: 'precluded by time.'

[110] Others consider the Means of Knowledge to be more than the three which the Vedāntins consider can cover all. The other Means (*Pramāṇas*) are such as:—*Upamāna* or Comparison, *Arthāpatti* or Assumption, *Sambhava* or Probability, *Aitihya* or Tradition; *Ceshṭā* or Gesture, *Abhāva* or Non-existence.

similar to that associated with cow. Then arises the knowledge of the form (or the new object, the Cow-like Gavaya), so associated, aided by the remembrance of the meaning of the sentence (before heard). Assortable thus with remembrance (memory), Comparison is classable under Perception.[111] Or it is classable under Inference as there is evidence of a process of induction (*Vyāpti*).[112] Or it may be surmised as falling under the class 'Word', for it is derived from a sentence (heard).

Arthâpatti or Assumption is thus:—A person is observed not eating in the day time, yet looks plump. The assumption is made that he eats in the night. This is classifiable under Inference.

Tarka or argument is the bringing about a non-desire (or negation) of the Pervading (*Vyāpaka*) by admitting the Pervaded (*Vyāpya*), thus:—Supposing an Inference were stated:

'The mountain is fiery
Because it is smoky';

---

[111] See Pages 14, 15, 16, 17 *ante.*

[112] I. e., Analogical reasoning.

and it were objected :—'Let there be smoke, but no fire', the argument would be: 'If there were no fire, let there be no smoke as well.'[113] The Means (*Pramāṇas*) promote this.[114]

Niścaya (Nirṇaya) or Ascertainment, is the ascertainment of a truth by the employment of Means, favoured by argumentation (*Tarka*).[115]

Vāda or Debate is unbiassed discussion, (or fair discussion by people free from prejudice).[116]

Jalpa or Wrangling is the discussion with the main view of (gaining) victory on either side.[117]

Vitaṇḍā or Cavilling, is the being devoid of (good reason for) establishing an opinion.[118]

Chala or Quibbling is the ascription of a different than the intended sense to an expression.[119]

---

[113] A *reductio ad absurdum*.

[114] Read *Gotama-Sūtra*: I. 1. 40: *Avigñāta* &c.

[115] " " " I. 1. 41: *Vimṛśya* &c.

[116] " " " I. 2. 42: *Pramāṇa* &c.

[117] " " " I. 2. 43: *Yathokto* &c.

[118] " " " I. 2. 44: *Sa-pratipaksha* &c.

[119] " " " I. 2. 54: *Sambhavato* &c.

Jāti or Futility is either reviling which will re-act on oneself, or a self-contradictory reply.[120]

Nigrahasthāna or that which courts one's own defeat.[121]

All these are but limbs of Inference; hence included in Inference.

We adopt the methods of the *Nāiyāyikas* wherever feasible. Hence such a course is not (to be thought) erroneous.

Thus has Inference been expounded.

Thus ends Advent II,
The Treatment of Inference (*Anumāna*)
in the
Light of the School of Rāmānuja.

---

[120] Read *Gotama-Sūtra*: I. 2. 56: *Sādharmya* &c.

[121] " " " I. 2. 60: *Vipratipatti* &c.

Nigrahasthāna, literally means 'Occasion for rebuke', 'Unfitness for argument' is the sense intended.

ADVENT III—THE WORD (*Šabda*).

After the exposition of Inference (*Anumāna*), the word (*Šabda*)[122] will be expounded.

Šabda-Pramāṇa or the Instrument (or Means) viz, 'Word', is that which produces the knowledge obtained from sentences non-uttered by the non-trustworthy (men) (*An-āptā*).[122] 'Non-uttered by the Non-trustworthy' is (a characterisation advisedly) employed to controvert the opinion that 'the Word' (*Vedas*) is of human origin. Or 'the Word' is that which is exempt from the sense-errors (*Karaṇa-dosha*)[123] and contrarieties (*Bādhaka-pratyaya*).[124]

---

[122] 'Word' means 'Holy' Word, Revelations or The Scriptures; or traditionary lore handed down by agents worthy of confidence = Vedas. Vide, *Āptopadešas Šabdaḥ*' [Sāṅkhya-Sūtras. I. 101].

[123] *I. e.*, errors arising from the defects of perceptive and active senses in persons,—the 'Personal equations'.

[124] *I. e.*, Opposing elements, such as intrinsic, extrinsic and commonsense contradictions.

At the outset of a Creation, God (*Bhagavān,*)[125] evolved out of His Consciousness what past order of the Vedas had there lain, and taught them to Catur-mukha.[126]. When this is granted, eternality and non-human-ness are assured. Then are absent the errors of sense and contrarieties.

But it may be asked how the *Vedas* can be authoritative (*Prāmāṇyam*), inasmuch as the Mīmāṁsakas[127] admit them only as concerned with *Kārya* or Effects, and that Texts concerning the Self-evident (*Siddha*) Brahman (God),

---

[125] Personal God. See J. R. A. S. for July 1910 for a discussion of the term *Bhagavān.*

[126] The Demiurge or the Four-faced First Lord of Creation. The four faces uttered the Four Vedas.

[127] The School of the Vedas who contend that work is Deity, and work done generates Effects, or whatever Fruits are desired by mankind. Hence these are said to belong to the 'Effects' faction. *Per contra* are the Vedāntins who posit Brahman or God as the 'Effective' or ready, or what is Self-Evident (*Siddha*), and that Holy Vedic Texts need not necessarily be with reference to 'Effects' but they as well educate or instruct mankind as to God, a self-evident fact, or a fact not 'effectible' or 'creatable' as the Mīmāṁsakas would contend.

do not convey instruction. This (objection) is met by showing that (1) these Texts which are concerned with the Self-evident Brahman are employable for purposes of contemplation (*Upāsana*), partaking of the nature of effects (*Kārya*); (2) that even sentences employed in wordly affairs, such as: 'Thy father is doing well,' do convey instruction (or sense); and (3) that in the world it is seen that children, gradually and repeatedly taught by their mothers, fathers *etc.*, by employing words connoting mother, father, uncle, moon *etc.*, (at same time) indicating these with their fingers, come to understand the meanings thereof: Hence, in the (case of the) Vedas also, words convey instruction (or knowledge) of things self-evident. Hence there is no room for questioning the authoritativeness of the Vedas.

(Also) it need not be doubted how that part (of the Vedas) which treats of *Abhicāra etc.*,[128] can be authoritative, for by their means visible

[128] Spells, Incantations and such other thaumaturgical work employed for malevolent purposes, such as for killing an enemy &c.

results are demonstrated that thus, an incentive for engaging in works fructescent of invisible results, such as *Svarga etc.*,[129] may be provided.

Such texts as: "Post-Sun"[130] are construable as meaning that the Post is as shining as the Sun.

Hence in their totality are the *Vedas* authoritative.

This Veda is twofold: (1) the Pre-Division (*Pūrva*) treating of Works (*Karma*),(2) the Post-Division (*Uttara*) treating of God (*Brahman*).

The Pre-Division treats of Works, which is Worship (of God); and the Post-Division treats of Brahman (God), the Worshippable. Hence both the *mīmāṁsas*, or Vedic Discourses constitute one Science (*Śāstra*).

---

[129] Paradise, material heavens.

[130] Post is the Sacrificial Post fixed in the Sacrificial Yard (*Yāga-Śāla*) for tying the victims. 'Post-Sun' is a metaphor meaning that the Post is as bright as the Sun, not the Sun itself, which would be absurd, and therefore Veda itself absurd. [*Vide Jaiminīya-Nyāya-Mālā*. I. 4. 15, and *Kṛshṇa-Yajur-Brāhmaṇa*. I. 2. 5].

Comprised of the Two Divisions, (the Vedas) are made up of Ṛg, Yajus, Sāma and Atharvaṇa.

These again branch out innumerable.

The diversified Ṛg. *etc.*,-Veda is three-fold, such as *Mantra*, *Arthavāda* and *Vidhi*.

Mantra explains the Purpose (*artha*) of action, (or shows the motive for act).

Arthavāda constitutes passages intended to stimulate effort conformable to Injunctions (*Vidhi*).

Vidhi is 'text' which enjoins what is good (for one to do). *Vidhi* (Injunction) is again threefold:—

(1) *Apūrva*, (2) *Parisaṅkhyā* and (3) *Niyama*. Again is it divisible into many classes; such as: *Nitya*, *Naimittika*, *Kāmya* &c.

Apūrva-Vidhi comprises such injunctions as: 'Sprinkles paddy'.[131]

Viśishṭa-Vidhi (falling under Apūrva) is meditative injunctions such as *mano-maya*.[132].

---

[131] '*Vrīhin prokshati*':

[132] 'Mind-apprehensible', one of the attributes of God to be meditated on. This attribute is mentioned along with others. *Vide* Chhāndogya-Upanishat: III. 14. 2, and Vedānta-Sūtras; I. 2. 1*ff.*

Parisaṅkhyā-Vidhi comprises such injunctions as:—

'Holding this rope'.[133]

Niyama-Vidhi[134] comprises such injunctions as require (a disciple) approaching the holy preceptor.

Nitya-Vidhi comprises such injunctions as the twilight meditations (*Sandhyā-Vandana*).

Naimittika-Vidhi comprises such injunctions as the *Ishṭi*[135]-performances *etc.*, consequent on birth.

Kāmya-Vidhi comprises such injunctions as the performances of Jyotishṭoma[136] *etc.*

Thus the Veda comprised of *Vidhi*, *Arthavāda* and *Mantra*, has the limbs, (1) *Chhandas*,

---

[133] '*Imām agṛbhṇan raśanām*'. [Kṛshṇa-Yajus-Samhitā: V. 1. 2].

[134] This verse may be of use:—"*Vidhir antyantam aprāpto niyamaḥ pākshike sati, tatra cā'nyatra ca prāptau parisaṅkhyā vidhīyate.*"

[135] A sacrifice where butter &c. are oblated, and neither animal nor the *Soma*-plant.

[136] A Soma-Sacrifice typical of a whole class of Vedic ceremonies. Read "*Jyotish ṭomam prathamam upayanti*". [Kṛshṇa-Yajus-Samhitā: VII. 4. 11].

(2) *Kalpa* (3) *Śikshā*, (4) *Nirukta*, (5) *Jyotisha*, and (6) *Vyākaraṇa*.

Chhandas is the exposition (of metres) such as *Anushṭup*, *Trishṭup* &c. (Metrics).

Kalpa is the exposition of the *modus operandi* of Śrauta[137] and Smārta[138] ritual. *Śikshā* is what concerns itself with the syntactical collocation of letters (Phonetics).

Nirukta is what concerns itself with the explanation of rare meanings (of words) (Etymological lexicography).

Jyotisha is what determines the time for undertaking *Adhyayana* and its precepts (Astronomy and Astrology).

Vyākaraṇa is known to be that which determines the pure word-formation and intonation (Grammar).

Thus, the authoritativeness of the Veda with its limbs is evident (or established).

Smṛti[138] is authoritative, for it is not opposed to *Śruti*;[137] expounds (the Law of) *Ācāra* or

---

137 What belongs to *Śruti* or Vedas (what is *heard*).

138 " " " *Smṛti* or Dharma-Śāstras (what is *remembered* or what is *heard*. Hence the *Smṛtis* have their roots in the *Śruti*).

conduct, *Vyavahāra* or Transactions, *Prāyaś-citta* or Penances, *etc.*, and instituted by our *Āptas* or Elderly well-wishers.

Though Hiraṇyagarbha[139] and others are all well-meaning (*āpta*), they are subject to the influences of the Three Guṇas.[140] Hence those portions of their works: Yoga,[139] Kāpila[141] *etc.*, are alone authoritative which do not conflict with the *Smṛtis* of Manu and others; only those portions which contradict true tenets (*tattva*) are discarded.

The authoritativeness of *Itihāsas* and *Purāṇas*[142] are self-evident by reason of their Exegetic character on the Vedas.

As regards (Mahā-)Bhārata and Rāmāyaṇa[143]

---

[139] Same as *Caturmukha* or the four-faced Demiurge. The first authorship belongs to him of the Yoga-Śāstra. Pātañjala and other works are based upon that Original.

[140] The *Satva* (pure), *Rajas* (mixed) and *Tamas* (impure) properties of matter, which affect the mind as they happen to be each in the ascendant. See *Vedānta-Sūtras* II. 1. 1 *ff*:

[141] I. e. the Sāṅkhya System by Kapila.

[142] Means Old Chronicles.

[143] These works come under *Itihāsa*.

(*Itihāsas*), any passages or tenets which may seem objectionable must be duly interpreted in the same manner as the Vedānta-passages are.

The *Purāṇas* also, treating of the Five (Topics): creation *etc.*, are divisible into the (three) groups: *Sātvika* (pure), *Rājasa* (mixed) and *Tāmasa* (impure); and where they conflict with true tenet (*tattva*), they are no authority. The rest is authoritative.

The Pāśupata etc.,[144] *Āgamas* are likewise (to be considered).

The Pāñcarātra-Āgamas viz: *Āgama-*, *Divya-tantra-*, *Tantrāntara-*, *Siddhāntas*, are in their totality authoritative, for nowhere do they conflict with the Vedas. Likewise is the Vaikhā-nasa-*Āgama*.[145]

---

[144] Read *Vedānta-Sūt*: II. 2. 35. *Patyur* &c.

[145] " " " II. 2. 8. *Utpatti* &c. And also see our Article on *Pāñcarātra* in J. R. A. S. for October 1911. *Paushkara-Saṁhitā* enumerates four divisions: *Āgama*, *Mantra*, *Tantra* and *Tantrāntara*, all of them being Doctrine (*Siddhānta*). Read Vedāntâcārya's Work: The *Pāñcarātra-Rakshā* for details.

Likewise are the Dharma-Šāstras.* The Law-Makers are Šāṇḍilya, Parāšara, Bhāradvāja, Vasishṭha, Hārīta and others.

Likewise, where requisite, are the *Šilpa* (Architectonics), *Āyur-Veda* (Life-knowledge, i. e. Medicine), *Gāndharva* (Music) etc.

Šilpa is the treatise on the subject of foundation, construction of turrets, enclosures *etc.* *Āyur-Veda* is medicine; *Gāndharva* treats of music *etc.* Of this the Bharatâ-"gama deals with (the art of) dancing.

Also amongst the sixty-four Crafts,[145] whatever is useful for *Tattva* (Truth), *Upāya* (Means) and *Purushārtha* (Goal), is authoritative.

More authoritative are the Blessed Utterances of such saints as Vakuḷâ-"bharaṇa.[146]

---

* Social, legal and religious polity of the Hindus.

[145] For an enumeration of these Crafts (*Kaḷās*), see Vāsudeva's commentary on Yatīndra-mata-Dīpikā, called *Prakāša* [Ānandâšrama Series, Pūna. No. 50].

[146] *Lit.*, the Vakuḷa-(*Mimusops Elengi*) decked, a name of St. Nammāzhvār, for whose life, see our *Lives of Drāvida Saints*. An enumeration of his works is also there to be found. These Treatises are all in Tamil poetry, called *Prabandhas*.

8

Most authoritative are the works composed by Blessed Teachers (*Ācāryas*) such as Rāmānuja, viz., Śrī-Bhāshya[147] *etc.*

Paurusheya or of 'human origin' are works characterised by their dependence on the free-will of man and by (merit of) singular composition. In this definition is included all such works as *Kāvya* or poetics, *Nāṭaka* or Histrionics, *Alaṅkāra* or Rhetorics.

As authoritative likewise are worldly utterances by (our) well wishers (*āpta*) which possess (the features of) (1) *Ākāṅkshā*,[148] (2) *Yogyatā*[149] and (3) *Āsatti*;[150] for example when it is said:

[147] The Great Commentary on the Vedānta-Sūtras, expounding the *Viśishṭâ-'dvaita* philosophy and religion. For Rāmānuja's History and his works, see our LIFE OF RĀMĀNUJA.

[148] *Lit.*, 'desiring', or that which desires a word or words, by the supply of which a sense desired to be conveyed is made complete. 'Horse', if uttered singly, desires for other words.

[149] *Lit.*, 'fitness', or that which conveys a reasonable sense. 'Horse talks' for example would be absurd.

[150] *Āsatti* or *Sannidhi* is *lit.*, Proximity or Juxtaposition. Where 'Horse' is uttered at one time,

'The river-side abounds with five kinds of fruit.'

Thus (also) both the Vedic as well as the (Laukik) worldly utterances have a property common to them again, which is twofold: (1) *Mukhya-vṛtti* or Primary force, and (2) *Gauṇa-vṛtti* or Secondary force.

Mukhya-vṛtti or Primary force is the *Abhidhā-vṛtti*[181] or denotative power, for example (the word) 'Lion', denoting (or meaning) the 'King of the Forest' (only). The Primary power (of words) is further resolvable into many varieties such as: *Yoga* or Radical (or etymological), *Rūdha* or Conventional, and *Yoga-rūdha* or Radical-Conventional,* etc.

Where the Primary force is affected, the next nearest sense becomes the metaphorical (*Upacāra*).

---

and 'neighs' after a long interval, it would be wanting in that Proximity which would convey the sense: 'Horse neighs.' [See *Tarka-Saṁgraha*, *Dīpikā* &c].

[181] See *Sāhitya-Darpaṇa*; *Kāvya-prakāśa* &c.

* The word "*Pankaja*" for example, which means lotus, for it grows up from mire.

The Metaphorical is again divisible into: (1) *Lakshaṇā* or Indirect and (2) *Gauṇa* or Secondary. The First (*Lakshaṇā*) is thus: 'A hamlet in the Gaṅgā' means a hamlet on its bank, as, for a hamlet directly located (in the river itself of Gaṅgā) is a violation (of sense); hence indirectly the bank (of Gaṅgā) is meant. The second (*Gauṇa*) is thus:—'A lion is Devadatta', is to indicate that Devadatta is endowed with strength *etc.*, (like the lion).

Thus all utterances, Vedic and of the world, have reference to objects with attributes, and import duality.[162]

As in the manner that terms denoting 'body' have their final connotation for the 'embodied,'[163]

---

[162] The author here alludes to the *Advaitic* or monistic doctrine which disproves duality or all distinctions or differences actually discernible in Nature.

[163] I. e., the Possessor of the body, or the living spirit or soul in the body. When I say 'I', pointing to my body, the term 'I' means eventually the soul in the body. By parity of reasoning, all terms which denote the Kosmos refer finally to the Substrate or Noumenon which sustains it, without which Kosmos can have no existence. Hence Kosmos is 'Body' to God, and God is therefore the 'Embodied'.

so all 'Soul'-terms denoting Brahma, Rudra, Agni, Indra &c., constituting the 'Body' of God (*Bhagavān*), and similarly 'Non-soul' terms denoting Matter (*Prakṛti*), Time (*Kāla*), Ether (*Ākāša*), Life (*Prāṇa*) etc., all have their final connotation in the 'Embodied', The Supreme Spirit (*Paramātman*), Nārāyaṇa. [184] Thus do the Teachers (*Ācāryas*) propound. The ultimate import of all Vedāntic Sentences is understood as thus interpreted.

We shall in the Advent (IX) on Īšvara (God), discourse on (the topic of) Nārāyaṇa,[184] as the Ultimate Connotee of all terms, His All-bodied Character *etc.*

Thus ends Advent III.
The Treatment of Word (*Šabda*)
in the
"Light of the School of Rāmānuja".

[184] The conception of God as conveyed by this term is elaborately treated in the 'Rahasyas' of the Višishṭâdvaitins. Our own works in English explain it in diverse places. Briefly the sense may be gathered from the passage in the *Nārāyaṇ-opanishat*: "Antar bahiš ca tat sarvam vyāpya Nārāyaṇas sthitaḥ."

ADVENT IV.
OBJECT OF KNOWLEDGE
(*Prameya*).

MATTER (*Prakṛti.*)

After the treatment of Pramāṇa (or Means of knowledge) Prameya [155] or Object of knowledge will be treated. *Prameya* (literally) means what is well (*pra*), measured (*meya*).

It (Object) is twofold: *Dravya* or Substance, and *A-dravya* or Non-Substance. Substance is the *Upādāna* or Substrate, Base or Receptacle; and the Receptacle is the Abode of States or Modes (*Avasthâ-"śraya*).

How, it may be asked, is this twofold division: Substance and Non-Substance to be maintained, when other schools enumerate a six-fold division:—*Dravya* or Substance, *Guṇa* or Quality, *Karma* or action, *Sāmānya* or Genus *etc*? [156]

---

[155] *Lit.*, *Pramāṇa* = Measure (i. e. Proof or Demonstration). *Prameya* = Measured (i. e. the Proved or Demonstrated).

[156] According to the Categories of Nyāya Philosophy. The others are: *Viśesha* or Particularity,

We reply :

To consider *Karma* or Action (for example), as comprised of *Ut-kshepaṇa* or Throwing up, *Apa-kshepaṇa* or Throwing down, *Ākuñcana* or Contraction, *Prasāraṇa* or Expansion, and *Gamana* or Movement,[157] is cumbrous, for it is reducible to the simple proposition : 'Action (or Energy) is what is inherent with motion.' And this may be shown as caused by conjunction (*Saṁyoga*).[158]

As to *Sāmānya*, Genus or Generality, such (a category) is redundant by the fact that the form (of any substance) is itself the class (*Jāti*).

One *Samavāya* or Inhesion (or Co-inherence), admitted in another Inhesion, leads to infinite regress. Hence it is resolvable into conjunction (or quality of two things conjoined).'[159]

It is also cumbrous to admit (another Category): *Viśesha* or Particularity, in order to

---

Samavāya or Inhesion and *Abhāva* or Non-existence. With the last the number becomes seven ; *et seq.*

[157] *Vide, Tarka-Saṁgraha* &c.

[158] 'Conjunction' is one of the 24 Qualities of the Category *Guṇa* [*Vide. op. cit*].

[159] The 'Cohesion,' mechanical, chemical or molecular.

account for such differences of attributes as those of Atomicity (*Aṇutva*) and Infinitude (*Vibhutva*), characterising (respectively) Soul (*Jīva*) and God (*Īśvara*).

Hence, as distinct (Categories), Action (*Karma*), Generality (*Sāmānya*), Particularity (*Viśesha*) and Inhesion (*Samavāya*) are not admitted, the twofold Division: Substance (*Dravya*), and Non-Substance (*A-dravya*), answers well.

By this, it is also refuted that *Abhāva* (Non-existence) is a seventh Category; for Non-existence always implies its correlative, Existence (*Bhāva*).

Prāg-abhāva or antecedent Non-existence is previous condition; *Dhvaṁsa* or (post-cedent) destruction is the after-condition. *Atyantâ-"bhāva* or Absolute Non-existence, and *Anyonyâ-"bhāva* or Mutual Non-existence, (simply) refer to particular features in a Substance (*Dharmi*). Hence the inclusion of this (category, viz., *Abhāva*) under (*Pratyaksha* or) Perception.

It was said that *Dravya* (Substance) is the *Upādāna* (or Abode of States: *Avasthâ-"śraya*).

The general definition also holds good that Substance is the Abode of Attributes (*Guṇâ-"ŝ-raya*).

The Substances (then) are Six:—(1) *Prakṛti* or Matter, (2) *Kāla* or Time, (3) *Šudda-satva* or Pure Matter, (4) *Dharmabhūta-Jñāna* or attributive consciousness, (5) *Jīva* or Soul, and (6) *Īšvara* or God.[160]

These (Six Substances) are divisible into two classes, *Jaḍa* or Inert, and *A-jaḍa* or non-inert (i.e., Self-luminous).

The nature of the 'Inert' is described as that which is devoid of Non-mixed Matter.[161] And

[160] Of these (1) and (2) may be called *Objective Substance;* and (5) and (6) *Subjective Substance,* (3) and (4) linking the two sets. (3) may be called *Subjective Matter,* (1) being called *Objective Matter*; and (4) may be called *Conscious Substance.* Science has made a distinction between *Ponderable* matter and *Imponderable* matter; but the latter is still *Objective.* Hence (3) *Šuddha-Satva,* a matter which is of the celestial or heavenly order, is thus best conceivable by the expression *Subjective-matter.*

[161] Objective Matter is *Mixed* Matter; *Pure* Matter is Subjective Matter. That which is not the latter is the former which is *Inert* or that which is not Self-luminous.

this is of two kinds: *Prakṛti* or (objective) Matter, and *Kāla* or Time.

Prakṛti or (Objective or Mixed) Matter is the Abode of the Three *Guṇas* or Properties[168] viz., *Satva* (Light), *Rajas* (Motive) and *Tamas* (Dark). It is *Nitya* or Eternal, called by such names as *Aksharā* or the Imperishable, *Avidyā* or the Nescient, *Māyā* or the Illusory *etc.*

By reason of oddness produced in it (Matter) by the will of God (*Bhagavān*), it acquires a kinetic (*Kāry-onmukha*) state, which is called *Avyakta* or Indiscreet. From this, *Mahān* or 'Great' is produced. *Mahān* is in a threefold state, characterised by *Satva, Rajas* and *Tamas*. From *Mahat*, *Ahaṁkāra* or the 'Individualising' is generated. This also is in three divisions: *Sātvikâ'haṁkāra, Rājasâ'-haṁkāra* and *Tāmasâ'hâṁkāra*. These are otherwise also named as *Vaikārika, Taijasa* and *Bhūtādi* (respectively). Being known as *Vaikārika* or the Modifying, the *Sātvikâ'haṁkāra*

---

168 'Energies' may be a better term to suit the scientific sense of the age.

aided bythe *Taijasa*, named *Rājasâ'haṁkāra*, engenders the Eleven *Indriyas* or Senses.

The definition of Sense is that which has for its material basis the *Sātvikâ'haṁkāra*. The Sense is twofold, the *Jñān-endriya* or Knowledge-sense, and *Karm-endriya* or Action-sense. The Knowledge-sense is that by which knowledge is transmitted. It is sixfold : (1) *Manas* or mind, (2) hearing, (3) seeing, (4) smelling (5) tasting and (6) touch. The mind is that which causes memory (*smṛti*) *etc.* This resides in the region of the heart. It is variously called by the terms *Buddhi* or Intelligence, *Ahaṁkāra* or the 'I-making', *Citta* or Recollection *etc.* And it is the Cause of Bondage (*Bandha*) and Deliverance (*Moksha*) [168].

---

[168] *Manas* is the organ through which soul's consciousness flows to the Senses, and thus performs the *efferent* function, and again is it the *Sense Commune*, to which all the *afferent* sensations gathered by the avenues of the Ten Senses, those of Knowledge as well as those of Action, converge, and percepts, there formed into concepts, are delivered finally to the Soul. In Western Psychology, Mind includes soul and is the Principle of consciousness, whereas in Eastern Psychology, soul alone is

Of the (other) Five: hearing *etc.*, that which has the power of apprehending sound only, is the Sense of Hearing, which resides in the cavity of the Ear—the Eye in the case of serpents *etc.* That which has the power of apprehending color only, is the Sense of Seeing which resides in the Eye. That which has the power of apprehending Odour only, is the Sense of Smelling which resides in the nasal extremity—the trunk in the elephant *etc.* That which has the power of apprehending Savour only, is the Sense of Tasting which resides at the tip of the tongue. That which has the power of apprehending Touch only, is the Sense of Touch which resides all over the body. Touch, not (keenly) felt in nails, teeth, hair &c., is accounted for by degrees of the low vitality of those places. The description of

---

the Principle of Consciousness, rather the Abode of Consciousness; and mind is a material sense, internal, the external being the other ten senses: seeing *etc.*

The Division of this mind into Buddhi *etc.*, has only partial correspondence with the Western Division of Intellect, Will and Feelings. The mind residing in the heart has a bearing on the Feelings connected with this same organ.

the Senses of Hearing etc., as Elemental (*Bhautika*) is figurative by virtue of the Elements affording them gratification. Of these (senses) some function by (mediate) association, and some by (immediate) contact with objects. So avers old tradition.

The facility to act—any one out of them such as speaking *etc.*,—characterises generally the *Karm-endriya* or Action-Sense. This (Action-Sense) is established in a fivefold manner: Speaking, Grasping, Moving, Evacuating and Generating. That which enables articulation of letters is the Sense of Speaking. This abides in eight places, viz., heart, throat, tip of tongue, palate, teeth, lip, nose and head. In the case of mutes *etc.*, the defect of Destiny (or merit) accounts for its absence. That which enables manual work is the Sense of Grasping. This resides at the finger-tips of the human *etc.*, species. That which enables to move is the Sense of Moving. This resides in the feet of human and other species. In the case of serpents and birds *etc.*, it resides in the breast, wings *etc.* That which enables evacuation *etc.*, is the Sense of Evacuation. This resides in the several organs (*Pāyu*) set apart (for the purpose). That which causes a specific joy is the Sense of Generation. This resides in the organ of generation (*Upastha*)* *etc.* These Senses are minute[164]. These accompany the Soul (*Jīva*) in its migrations to other bodies and other worlds etc. In the state of emancipation (*mukti*), they cannot accompany to the immaterial regions; hence their abidance here till the Period of Dissolution; or they are reappropriated by others who stand in need of them. That the Senses of Action perish with the death of the body is an opinion contrary to *Bhāshya*[165] etc. Hence inadmissible. The opposite schools are also controverted, therefore, which maintain a male sense, a female sense, a single sense: the sense of Touch only *etc.*

---

* For a Tabulation of these results, consult pp. 257 & 258 of our *Bhagavad-Gītā*: Commentaries.

[164] Read *Vedānta-Sūtra*: II-4-6. 'Aṇavaś ca.'

[165] *I. e.*, *Śrī-Bhāshya* or Rāmānuja's Commentary on the Vedānta-Sūtras, and other works on the *Viśishṭâdvaita* philosophy.

From the *Tāmasâ'haṁkāra*, called *Bhūtādi* fostered by *Rājasâ'haṁkāra*, spring the five Subtle Elements (*Tanmātras*), Sound *etc*, and the Five Elements (*Bhūtas*), Ether etc. The Subtle Elements are the Subtle Substances immediately connected with the (gross) Elements; and they are the base (of the latter). Elements are the Substrata in which the objective Sound *etc*, inhere. The Subtle Elements are five:—

(1) Sound-Subtle Element, (2) Touch-Subtle Element, (3) Colour-Subtle Element, (4) Savour-Subtle Element, (5) Odour-Subtle Element. The Elements are also five:—(1) Ether, (2) Air, (3) Fire, (4) Water, (5) Earth.

The Sound-Subtle Element is the compound substance intervenient to *Tāmasâ'haṁkāra* and Ether (*Ākāśa*), like the modification between milk and curds. From this (Subtle Element) springs Ether. The properties of Ether are defined in such terms as:—

(1) Imperceptible to touch, is the Substrate for the quality Sound,

(2) Affording gratification to the Organ of hearing (Ear),

(3) Affording room (extension).

It (Ether) is characterised by Sound only. It is perceptible according to the familiar saying: 'Sky is blue'. It has color and parts by reason of the Quintuplicative Process (*Pañcī-karaṇa-Prakriyā*). By this (reasoning), the opinion that Ether is non-generate is disproved.

A distinct (Category such as) Direction (*Dik*) needs no creation, inasmuch as such Direction as East etc, is derivable from the associations of the motions of the sun with the sky (*Ākāśa*). The creation of Direction is to be understood like the creation of Sky *etc.*

From Ether springs the Touch-Subtle Element. This Touch-Subtle Element is the compound Substance occupying the intermediate state between Ether and Air. From it Air springs. The properties of Air are defined in such terms as:—

(1) Perceptible everywhere to touch, absent of color,

(2) The Substance perceptible to the Sense of Touch as we possess it,

(3) Neither warm nor cold to touch, absent of color. This Air is diverse. It receives the designation of cold, warm, fragrant *etc*, by virtue of its (Air's) contact with water, heat, flower *etc.*, (respectively). It is helpful to the Sense of Touch by its rendering it gratification. Its characteristics are Sound and Touch. And in its function of supporting the body, it is called *Prāṇa* or Life (Vital Air).

This (*Prāṇa* or Life) is fivefold: (1) *Prāṇa* (2) *Apāna*, (3) *Vyāna*, (4) *Udāna* and (5) *Samāna*. *Prāṇa* (resides) in the heart, *Apāna* in the anus, *Vyāna* pervades the body, *Udāna* (is) in the throat, and *Samāna* in the regions of the navel. This law holds in the case of the Movables (*Jaṅgama*). In the case of the Immovables (*Sthāvara*), the Life-association is slender. The contention that air is proved by Inference is confuted by the fact that it is perceptible to Touch.

The Color-Subtle-Element is the compounded substance intervenient to Air and Fire. From that springs Fire.

The definition of Fire is :—

(1) Warmth to touch,

(2) Lustrous coloredness.

It causes outside, maturing *etc.*, by means of Fire and Sun, and inside, as fire in the stomach, is designated as *Vaiśvānara:* Except in the case of owls *etc.*, all ocular knowlege is aided by means of light. This (Fire-Element) is fourfold: (1) *Bhauma*, (2) *Divya*, (3) *Audarya*, (4) *Ākar-aja*. That which is in the earthy fuel is *Bhauma* (terrestrial)—the flame *etc.* That which is of water only is *Divya* (celestial)—the Sun* *etc.* That which is in earth and water combined is *Audarya* (bodily),—the stomach-fire *etc.* Fuel-less fire is *Ākaraja* (mineral)—gold *etc.* The absence of warmth in the touch of gold (etc.,) is due to its association with other substances.

There is also a general classification as (1) Effulgence (*Prabhā*) and the Effulgent (*Prabhāvān*). Effulgence is a Fire-species which is subject to contraction or expansion of radiance caused by the presence or absence of

---

* *Etc.*, includes lightning and such other fiery Elements potentially abidant in the Water-Element.

environment (respectively). This Effulgence is connate with the Effulgent, and disappears with its disappearance. It is of the *substance*, as also of the *quality* and made up of parts. Hence the contention for its purely *qualitative* character, is refuted. Characterised by Effulgence is the Effulgent. That this (Fire-Element) is fourfold has already been explained. It is possessed of the qualities of Sound, Touch and Color.

The Savour-Subtle-Element is the compounded Substance intervenient to Fire and Water. From that springs Water. Its definition is given in such terms as:—

(1) Coldness to touch,

(2) Odourless and Savourful.

Its nature being white, sweet and cold, the differences of Color, Savour, and Touch are adventitious qualities ensuant on contact with extrinsic circumstances.

This (Water) is manifold as of the ocean, the river *etc.* It is characterised by Sound, Touch, Color and Savour. By it, is sprinkling, lumping *etc.*, (done).

The Odour-Subtle-Element is the compounded Substance which is intervenient to Water and Earth. Form it springs Earth. Its definition is given in such terms as:—

(1) All-odorous,

(2) Odorous, and neither warm nor cold to touch.

It is redolent, sweet, dark-coloured, and neither warm nor cold to touch. Its modifications bring about all kinds of Color, Odour and Savour. Its use is displayed by its affording gratification to mind and nose. Its modifications assume the character of mud, stone, food, herbs *etc.* It is characterised by the qualities: Sound Touch, Color, Savour and Odour. It is the means of support. Darkness is included in Earth, for it is its quality, or a particular state of it. Hence the opinion that it is merely the absence of light and not a substance *etc.*, is rebutted.

Consequent on the Quintuplicative Process (*Pañci-karaṇa-prakriyā*), all the qualities (Sound etc.,) are to be found in all the Elements. God (*Bhagavān*) creates the Elements by the

Quintuplicative Process, divides each Element into two portions, and reserving one portion, divides the other portion into four parts. He distributes these four parts, one for each of the other four Elements. When this is done with regard to all the (Five) Elements, each Element retains its own moiety, the other moiety being compounded of the parts of the other Elements. By reason of its own component (moiety) being greater, and of the other components being smaller, it is designated by the terms: Earth *etc.* The teaching of the Triplicatory Process in the Vedas means by implication the Quintuplicatory Process. Others posit a Septuplicatory Process by combining the Elements with (the principles) *Mahat* and *Ahaṁkāra*.

Of these (Principles of Matter), twenty four in number, the five Elements, *Prakṛti* (Primal Matter), *Mahat* and *Ahaṁkāra*, organise the Body (*Śarīra*). The Eleven Senses, enumerated separately—a set for each Soul (*Purusha*)—possess each body, like gems set in a jewel. One definition of Body is thus-wise given :—

It is a Substance in indiscerptible relation with the Soul, to which it is bound as the

Sustained (*Ādheya*), *Ordained* (*Vidheya*) and *Disposed* (*Šesha*). Each of these: 'Sustained,' 'Ordained' and 'Disposed' may be considered also as a threefold distinctive definition. A neutral (*taṭastha*) definition is that it is a Substance distinct from God (*Īšvara*) and His knowledge (*Jñāna*). Hence, the definitions attempted by others are discarded, such as :—

(1) The 'abode of action' is Body,

(2) The 'abode of Senses' is Body,

(3) The 'house of enjoyment' is Body,

(4) The 'aggregate of the limbs: head, hands, feet *etc.*,' is Body; *etc.*

The Body is twofold: Eternal and Non-Eternal. The Eternal is the Body of God (*Īšvara*) the pure Abode *etc.*, of the Three-Propertied Substance,[166] Time and Soul; and the natural Body assuming the shapes of the kite,[167] snake[168] *etc*: of the Eternal-celestials (*Nitya-Sūris*).[169] The Non-Eternal is twofold:

---

[166] *I.e. Satva-Rajas-and-Tamas*-characterised matter.

[167] Garuḍa,

[168] Ananta or Ādi-Šesha.

[169] Or Archangels.

Non-Karma[170]-made and Karma-made (*Karma-kṛta*). The First constitutes the forms of God[171] (*Īśvara*), Mahat *etc.*, and likewise forms assumed at will by Ananta, Garuḍa *Etc.*, (Archangels), the Freed (*Mukta*)[172] and God. The Karma-made (body) is also twofold; (1) will-prompted Karma-made, and (2) exclusively Karma-made. The former is as in the case of great souls like Saubhari.[173] For others, the other. Again there is a twofold general classification: (1) Immovable and (2) Movable. The Immovable are the rocks, trees, shrubs etc. The Movable is fourfold:—(1) Celestial (*Deva*), (2) Human (*Manushya*), (3) Animal (*Tiryak*) and (4) Hellish (*Nāraki*). A division also is based upon the modes of birth: (1) seed-born, (2) sweat-born, (3) egg-born (oviparous) and (4) womb-born

170 Karma is the sum of acts generated by the soul, and constitutes the cause for embodied existence; and this *Karma* is spread over many such lives till enfranchisement (*Moksha*) is achieved.

171 I. e. the forms of *the body* of God.

172 *Vide* J R A S. pp. 573 *ff.* for July 1910.

173 Read *Vishṇu-Purāṇa* for his story, and Piḷḷai Lokācārya's *Tattva-traya*.

(viviparous).[174] Bodies born by no mode also exist.[175]

Thus the Egg[176] is generated by the Quintuplicative Process. The creation prior to that of the Egg is the General (*Samashṭi*) Creation, and after it is the Special (*Vyashṭi*) creation. Creation or birth, of *Mahat etc.*, means a change of state simply, as may be illustrated by the palm-leaf changing into the ear-ring[177], or as (is evident) in such expression as: army, forest [178] etc. The distinctions made in practice between Cause and Effect is consequent on a particular relation which holds between an antecedent and a postcedent state. Naming as a new category (*tattva*) is contingent on the abandonment of a

---

[174] *I. e.*, (1) *Udbhij-ja*, (2) *Sveda-ja*, (3) *Aṇḍa-ja*, (4) *Jarāyu-ja*. (1) may perhaps be latinized as granoparous and (2) as thermoparous.

[175] *I. e.*, Spontaneous generation, like the Aphides.

[176] *I. e.*, the Mundane Egg called the *Brahmāṇḍa* or a system containing 14 Worlds or Planes.

[177] The palm leaf is split, rolled and inserted in a hole made in the lobe of the ear by Hindu women. Also read *Vedānta-Sūtra*; III. 2. 2-26: 'Ubhaya &c.'

[178] *I. e.*, army is but a collection of men, and forest a collection of trees.

previous, and assumption of an after, mutation. This (process of naming) is continued down to (the category) Earth.

In this manner, the Twenty-four Categorical Divisions (of *Prakṛti*) consisting of Primal Matter, *Mahat*, *Ahaṁkāra*, the Eleven Senses, the Five Subtle Elements and the Five (Gross) Elements, have been described. Hence those outsiders (*Bāhyas*)[179] and *Pāśupatas*[180], who predicate a greater or a lesser number of Categories, are disregarded, as well as those who plead for the atomic theory (of the Universe).'[181]

The Primordial Matter *etc.*, constitute the Objects (*Bhogya*), Instruments (*Bhog-ôpakaraṇa*) and the Habitat (*Bhoga-sthāna*) of enjoyment for both God (*Īśvara*) and Soul (*Jīva*). The Objects are the group of things, of sound *etc.*

[179] *I.e.* those who are beyond the pale of the Vedic Authority; the heretics, so to say.

[180] *I.e.* those who predicate *Paśu-pati* or *Śiva* as the Lord of the Universe, which is opposed to the School of the Vedānta, *vide*: Brahma-Sūtra II. 2. 35: *Patyur asāmañjas syāt.*

[181] The *Vaiśeshika* School which posits atoms as the basis of the kosmos.

The Instruments are those of the Eye *etc.* The Habitat consists of the Egg (*Brahmāṇḍa*) *, composed of the Fourteen Spheres. The Egg is likened to a wood-apple, a result of the Quintuplicated Elements and of *Prārabdha* (or the sum of the Karmic forces set agoing by the countless souls whose destiny is linked with this particular Egg or System of world-process).

(The description of it is) thus:—*Bhū* is like the lotus. The *Mēru* is like the pericarp. To the South of Mēru are (situate) the *Varshas*: Bhārata, Kimpurusha, and Hari. To the North are the *Varshas*: Ramyaka, Hiraṇyaka and Mēru. To the East is the *Varsha* Bhadrāśva. To the West is the *Varsha* Ketumāla. In the Centre is the Iḷāvṛta. Composed of these Nine *Varshas* is the Jambū-Dvīpa, a lac of *yojanas*† in extent, enclosed by the Salt-Sea of equal extent. This Sea is begirt by the Plaksha-Dvīpa of double that extent composed of seven *Varshas*. This is (enclosed) by the Syrup[182]-Sea. This Sea by the Śālmali-Dvīpa. This again by

* See note (176), page 80.

† About 9 miles.

[182] *Lit.*, Sugar-cane-juice (*Ikshu*).

the Liquor-Sea. This by the Kuša-Dvipa. This by the Ghee[183]-Sea. This by the Krauñca-Dvīpa. This by the Curds-Sea. This again by the Šāka-Dvīpa. This again by the Milk-Sea. This is surrounded by the annular Pushkara-Dvīpa, made up of two *Varshas* and containing the mountain Mānasottara. This by Pure-Water-Sea. Each following Dvīpa [184] is to be considered as double (in extent of the preceding). The Plaksha *etc.*, Dvīpas contain Seven *Varshas*. This of the Seven *Varshas* is encircled by the Land of Gold, double its extent. The Land of Gold, by the Mountain Lokāloka. This Mountain by Tamas (Darkness?). Tamas by Uterine Waters[185]. Then the (spherical) Egg-Shell. Located below *Bhū* as thus (described), are the Seven *Lokas* or Realms named (1) Atala,

---

[183] *I.e.*, Clarified butter.

[184] *Lit*., Island. The conception of this is a Sphere having many concentric *i.e.*, insular, shells or bands of varying depths alternately solid and liquid. The *Varshas* are the Divisions in the shells situated in various directions, or surfaces of the shell-sphere. The aggregate of all these is called *Bhū* (not our single Earth as is commonly understood.)

[185] See page 84.

(2) Vitala, (3) Sutala, (4) Talātala, (5) Mahātala, (6) Rasātala, (7) Pātāla. Below (these) are the Hades (*Narakas*). They are Raurava and others, the chief being twenty one,—regions (allotted) for the sufferings of the sinful. Beyond is (again) Uterine[186] waters enclosed by egg-shell. A lac of *yojanas* beyond *Bhū* is the Sun-Sphere. This is *Bhuvar-Loka*. Beyond, is the Moon-Sphere. Beyond, the Star-Sphere. Beyond, the Mercury-and Venus-Spheres. Beyond, the Mars-, Jupiter-, Saturn-, and the Seven-Ṛshi-Spheres. Beyond (comes) the *Dhruva-Loka* (North Pole). All this (i. e., from the Sun-Sphere up) is the (*Svar-loka*). Beyond fourteen lacs (of *yojanas*), the *Mahar-loka* is a crore of *yojanas* in extent. Double that is *Jano-loka*. Qaudruple that is *Tapo-loka*. Beyond is *Satya-loka*, ten crores in extent. Beyond (again come) *Tamas*, Uterine[186] Waters and the Egg-shell. Thus the extent of *Bhū* is stated to be fifty crores of *yojanas*, in breadth and depth. The assertion that its extent is one-

---

[186] *Lit*., *Garbh-odaka*. The conception is that of the Egg as above described floating like the embryo in the uterine fluids.

hundred crores of *yojanas* is because of the differences in measure-standards. The Egg-Shell is a crore of *yojanas* in extent. Ten times this is the environment round the Egg (= a System). Eggs of this description without number are like water-bubbles, simultaneously projected by God (*Īśvara*). God's creation up to the four-faced Brahmā is *immediate*, thence-forward *mediate*. Such is the division. For enlargement (of this topic), the Gem of Purāṇas (i.e. *Vishṇu*-P) may be consulted. Thus Matter (*Prakṛti*) has been treated.

Thus ends Advent IV.
The Treatment of Matter (*Prakṛti*)
in the
"Light of the School of Rāmānuja".

ADVENT V.—TIME (*Kāla*).

Now, the species of the Non-Conscient (*Acit*), viz., Time, will be treated. Time is (an) inert (substance) devoid of the triad of *guṇas*.[186] It is eternal and infinite. It is triply divisible as Past, Future and Present. It is the time (element) indicated by such terms as Simultaneous, Immediate, Gradual *etc*; and is that which constitutes what is in vogue (as time-measures), viz., *Nimesha, Kāshṭhā, Tatparā, Vināḍi, Kalā, Ghaṭikā, Muhūrta*,[187] Day, Half-month, Month, Season, Solstice, Year *etc.* One month by human measure is a day for the *Pitṛs*, whose midday is the New-Moon day The period of a Manu covers seventy one

---

[186] I.e., *Satva, Rajas* and *Tamas*. See note 162, *p.* 66, and (my) Bhagavad Gītā. *p.* 67.

[187] 48 minutes = 1 *Muhūrta*.

24 minutes = 1 *Ghaṭikā*.

Kalā varies from 8 to 60 seconds.

Kāshṭhā = 1/30 *Kalā* = say 2 seconds.

Nimesha = Twinkling of the eye.

Vināḍi = 24 seconds.

Tatparā = Used in *Jyotisha* for 1/30 part of a *Nimesha*.

(*Amāvāsya*). One year by human measure is a day for the *Devas*, whose (half) day is the North-(summer) solstice, and night the South-(winter) solstice. Measured thus by the Devas' standard, twelve thousand years is called the Four Yugas. Four thousand of these constitutes *Kṛta-Yuga*, when Virtue (*Dharma*) is of its full measure. Three thousand of them with three parts of Virtue constitutes the *Treta-Yuga*. Two thousand with two parts of Virtue constitutes the *Dvāpara*. One thousand with one part of Virtue is the *Kali-Yuga*. Two thousand make up the interim periods (between the Yugas).[188] The period which makes a day of Brahmā is a thousand of these Four-*Yugas*; and a night (is) of equal duration. A day of Brahmā covers (the period of) fourteen Manus, likewise of the Indras and the Seven Ṛshis.

---

[188] Distributed thus:—

800 years between *Kṛta* and *Treta*.
600 years between *Treta* and *Dvāpara*.
400 years between *Dvāpara* and *Kali*.
200 years between *Kali*, and *Kṛta* next.
2000

See note 1 *p.* 275, (my) Bhagavad-Gītā.

Four-*Yugas*. Thus, measured by the standard of Brahmā, one hundred years is his life-length. All this is subject to Time. Likewise is subject to Time the various Dissolutions (*Praḷayas*): *Nitya* (frequent), *Naimittika* (occasional), *Prākṛta* (material), *etc.*[189] For time as Effect, Time itself is the Cause. Infinite time is eternal; finite times are non-eternal. Time so delineated constitutes an ingredient for God's (cosmic) Sport (i. e. Display). In the *Līlā-Vibhūti*,[190] God (*Īśvara*) works, subject to Time. Although Time exists in the *Nitya-Vibhūti*,[191] it is so by His will. Some say that time non-exists, others

---

[189] 1. *Nitya-Praḷaya* = Sleep or Death.

2. *Naimittika-Praḷaya* = Disintegration at every Brahmā's day.

3. *Prākṛta-Praḷaya* = Disintegration at every Brahmā's age.

4. *Ātyantika-Praḷaya* = Final Deliverance or Escape from all material trammels = *Moksha* = Salvation = Spiritual Goal Eternal. [Read *Vishṇu-Purāṇa*, VI. 3. 1 and 2: *Sarveshām* etc.]

[190] Means: Temporal Manifested Universe, the Sport wherein consists of the three acts of Creation, Sustenance and Destruction.

[191] This is the Eternal or Spiritual Universe of Ineffable Glory (= *Vibhūti*).

aver that *Tāmasa-Mahān* (a category of Matter) is time. But both these positions are contrary to Word (*Āgama*, i.e. Scriptures) and Perception (*Pratyaksha*). The Ācāryas[102] affirm that Time is a cognition by the Six Senses (i.e. Mind and the Five Senses of Knowledge); that it is an object of Inference is therefore rejected.

Thus has Time been treated.

Thus ends Advent V,
The Treatment of Time (*Kāla*)
in the
"Light of the School of Rāmānuja".

****

[102] Spiritual Preceptors, in a generic sense; the expositors and exegetists who came into prominence in South India, in a specific sense.

ADVENT VI.

SPIRITUAL UNIVERSE.

(*Nitya-Vibhūti*).

Now (the Subject of the) Spiritual Universe (*Nitya-Vibhūti*) will be propounded. Non-inertness (*Ajaḍatva*) is a property common to (the Principles:) Pure Matter (*Šuddha-satva*),[193] the Attributive Consciousness (*Dharma-bhūta-Jñāna*),[194] Soul (*Jīva*) and God (*Īšvara*). Non-inertness means Self-luminousness (*Svayam-prakāšatva*). Self-luminousness *cum* exteriority (*Parāktva*),[195] characterises both Pure Matter and Attributive Consciousness. *Satvam* or Lightness means that which, while self-luminous, is luminant to others. *Šuddha-Satvam*

---

[193] or Spiritual (Divine) Matter in the Spiritual Universe.

[194] *I. e.* Consciousness which is the intrinsic or inherent quality of the Soul. *Read* Advent VII, *infra*.

[195] Exteriority means the quality of illuminating other things, not self-luminous, the term self-luminous or Interiority being adopted as the equivalent for *Pratyaktva*.

or Essential lightness is to be Luminant, while distinct from the Tri-featured Substance,[196] or that specific uniqueness, which prevails in regions entirely exempt of Nescience (*Avidyā*).[197] This (spiritual) Universe is unbounded above and bounded below, non-conscient and self-luminous. It is called by the name Bliss (*Ānanda*), for it is the medium of bliss. As it is indicated by the *Pañcopanishan-Mantras*,[198] it is of the nature of the *Pañcopanishads*. Constituted as it is of the Five Spiritual (or Immaterial) Energies, it is said to be of that Five-Energied nature.[198] This Universe becomes

[196] This is the Material of the Material Universe, the genesis of which has been described in Advent IV. '*Prakṛti*.' The 'features' are the *Guṇas*.

[197] Nescience or Ignorance is the root of all evil. 'Where this is entirely absent' is a negative definition of the Kingdom of Heaven, i.e, the Spiritual Universe.

[198] Read the *Pañcarātras*. For the subject-matter here alluded to, *vide* Pādma-tantra : XII-36 *ff* beginning: "*Yojanānām koṭir ūrdhve*" &c. Vishṇu Himself is the Five-Spiritual-Energied Being according to the verse (*loc cit.*): "*Pañca-śakti-mayo Vishṇuḥ koṭi-yojana-sammite, āste Śrī-Bhūmi-sahito Vainateyena sevitaḥ.*" The five are named thus :—(1) *Sarva*, (2) *Nivṛtti*, (3) *Viśva*, (4) *Purusha* and (5) *Parameshṭhi*.

the Objects, Instruments and Places of enjoyment to God and to the Eternals (*Nitya*)[199] and the Freed (*Mukta*) (*Souls*), by God's will. Objects signify Fortune, *etc.*, Instruments: Perfumes, Flowers, Robes, Companions (*Vadhū*), Ornaments, Weapons *etc*; Places; Terraces, Ramparts, Pavilions, Air-Cars (*Vimāna*), Parks and Lotus-decked Ponds.

By God's eternal will (*Nity-ecchā*) are determined the (beatific) bodies of God and of the Eternals and the Freed (souls). By God's will (*Saṁkalpa*) alone are made the bodies of the Freed, the creation of Pitṛs *etc.*, for them, the assumption of numerous bodies simultaneously *etc.* The bodies of God in His *Vyūha*, *Vibhava* and *Arcâ'-vatāra* manifestations[200] are of the immaterial (*i.e.*, spiritual) nature. In the case of the *Arcâ'vatāra*, (or Images consecrated in Temples) the spiritual body, by God's grace won by propitiation, incarnates (in the Images)

[199] Those, Archangels or Powers or Hierachies who are ever of the Divine or Celestial order, and who never fall into Samsāra, thereby becoming *Baddhas* or Souls in material bondage.

[200] *Vide* P: 576 ff., JRAS., July, 1910.

after the vitalising (*Prāṇa-pratishṭhā*) process. 'How can happen a junction, between the material and the immaterial?' need not raise a doubt, for the doubt is cleared when it is shown that this is illustrated by the (spiritual) bodies of Incarnations as of Rāma and Kṛshṇa,—authoritative (-ly known to us).[201] The assumption of bodies by the Freed (*Muktas*) is solely for the service of God, for His pleasure, like the mask donned on occasions of festivals like the *Vasant-otsava*.[202] The expression: 'Six-Qualitied' is employed for God's body by reason of its manifesting the Six Qualities.[203] The glories of the Blessed Divine Figure (or Beatific Presence) consist of Resplendence (*Aujjvalya*), Beauty (*Saundarya*), Redolence (*Saugandhya*), Tenderness (*Saukumārya*), Loveliness (*Lāvaṇya*), Juvenility (*Yauvana*),

---

[201] Cf. Bhagavad-Gītā: *Avajānanti Mām mūdhāḥ mānushīm tanum āśritam, param bhāvam ajānanto Mama bhūta-mahēśvaram*". (IX. 11).

[202] Indian festivities when costumes are worn as in a fancy-dress ball.

[203] The Six Qualities are *Jñāna*, *Śakti*, *Bala*, *Aiśvarya*, *Vīrya* and *Tejas*., (See Rāmānujas' Introduction to *Bhagavad-Gītā*, my English Translation.)

Softness (*Mārdava*) etc., (all) of the nature of eternal, faultless and surpassing. Its excellency is evident from such works as Gītā.

Texts, which declare that the Freed (*Mukta*-soul) has no body, signify the negation of Karma-determined body.[204] The senses (in this body) being eternal, the law of Cause and Effect does not prevail. Hence like the material (series), it needs no distinct categorising. The school therefore which upholds a bodiless condition there (i.e., in the state of Mukti, or Freedom Spiritual) is thus rejected. Likewise the faction, which contends that it (the Eternal Universe, *Nitya-vibhūti*) is a portion of Matter, is also dismissed as it is in contravention of the passage: 'Beyond Darkness'[205]—that it is distinct from (*Ākāśa*) is proved by its properties of Sound, Touch, Colour, Savour and Odour, being of immaterial nature. That it is inert is

[204] That is: the body of bondage. From this there is escape, but the Freed or Saved soul can attire itself in any desired form of a celestial body. Karma is the sum of accumulated acts which fructify necessarily, like seeds sown necessarily sprout.

[205] 'Tamasaḥ parastāt' (*Muṇḍak-opanishat*, II. 2. 6).

disproved by its being of the self-luminous nature (*jñānâ-"tmakatva*).

The Spiritual, Divine, Blessed Figure of God (*Bhagavān*) is the repertory of all the contents (signified) in the Chapter on Weapons and Ornaments.[306] It is thuswise:—*Kaustubha*-Gem represents *Purusha* (Soul); *Śrī-vatsa*, Matter; the Club (*Gadā*), Mahat; the Conch (*Śaṅkha*), *Sātvikâ-'haṁkāra*; the Bow (*Śārṅga*), *Tāmasâ-haṁkāra*; the Sword (*Asi = Nandaka*), Knowledge; its Sheath, A-knowledge; the Discus (*Cakra*), mind; the Arrows, the Knowledge *cum* Action-Senses: the Garland (*Vanamālā = Vaijayanti*), the Subtle and Gross Elements. In this connection the following laconic verse is worthy of contemplation:

"*Cetaś cakrati cetanâ-'sir amatis tat-saṁvṛtir, mālikā bhūtāni svaguṇair ahaṁkṛti-yugam śaṅkhena sārṅgāyate, bāṇāḥ khāni dasā'pi kaustubha-maṇir jīvaḥ pradhānam punaś śrī-vatsam Kamalāpate tava gadām āhur mahāntam budhāḥ.*"[307].

---

[306] Read Ch. 22, Aṁśa 1., *Vishṇu-Purāṇa*.

[307] This needs no translation as its very paraphrase has just preceded it. Venkaṭâcārya in his *Vedānta-Kārikâvaḷi*, ascribes this verse to Vedānta-Deśika.

This Universe (Spiritual) is fourfold:—*Āmoda*, *Pramoda*, *Sammoda* and *Vaikuṇṭha*.[208] Again it is infinite-fold. It is designated by several cognomens such as: Tripād-Vibhūti, Parama-pada, Parama-vyoma, Parama-"kāśa, Amṛta, Nāka, Aprākṛta-Loka, Ānanda-Loka, Vaikuṇṭha, Ayodhyā *etc.*

In this Universe is situate the City of Vaikuṇṭha, with Seven Enclosures, and abounding in countless cupolas and ramparts. In it is the Divine Mansion named Ānanda. In it is constructed a Hall called Maṇi-Maṇḍapa, supported by innumerable pillars made of precious stones. In it is (the Seat) Ananta of the Thousand Hoods, dazzling, carrying the Divine Throne of the composition: Dharma[209] *etc.* On it is the Eight-Petalled Lotus, served (on either side) by (maidens) Vimalā *etc*, holding fans (the

---

[208] Āmoda = the Realm of Saṅkarshaṇa
Pramoda = „ „ „ Pradyumna
Sammoda = „ „ „ Aniruddha
Vaikuṇṭha = „ „ „ Vāsudeva

[209] *Dharma*, *Jñāna*, *Vairāgya* and *Aiśvarya*. The four legs of the Throne are said to be *A-dharma*, *A-jñāna*, *A-vairāgya* and *An-aiśvarya*.

insignia of Royalty) in their hands. Seated on it (the Lotus) is Šesha, the Seat of Supreme Wisdom and Strength.[210] Over (*Šesha*) is the Great Being who is beyond speech.[211]

Thus (the subject of) *Nitya-Vibhūti* or the Spiritual Universe has been treated.

Thus ends Advent VI,
The Treatment of *Nitya-Vibhūti*,
or The Spiritual Universe,
in the
" Light of the School of Rāmānuja ".

---

[210] Read verse 40, Yāmunâ"cārya's Stotra-Ratna: *Tayā sahâ "sinam* etc.

[211] The whole of the 12th Chapter in Bk. I of the Pāñcarātra: *Pādma-tantra*, may with advantage be perused in this connection.

ADVENT VII.

ATTRIBUTIVE CONSCIOUSNESS.

(*Dharma-bhūta-jñāna*).

Consecutively, (the topic of) Attributive Consciousness [212] will now be expounded. The nature of it is described thus:—

1. While it is self-luminous, non-sentient substance, it is 'objectivated' (*sa-vishayatvam*) (i.e., some object always constituting its content);

2. While it is pervasive (*Vibhu*), it is of the nature of substance (*Dravya*), and attribute (*Guṇa*) like light;

3. It is the illuminant of objects;

4. It is Intellect or Intelligence (*Buddhi*) *etc.*

Attributive Consciousness[212] is, to God and the Eternals (*Nityas*), ever eternal and pervasive (or diffusive); to the Bound (*Baddha*-souls) it

---

[212] *I. E.*, Consciousness which is an attribute of, or adjectival to, Soul or God. To translate *manas* by mind or equate mind with Consciousness are both erroneous, see note 221 *infra*.

is obstructed. To the Freed (*Mukta*-souls), it was before obstructed but now risen.

But it may be asked how, if Consciousness is eternal, the parlance such as: 'Consciousness is (now) born, Consciousness (now) lost' is to be accounted for? The answer is that such is in vogue by reason of Consciousness being susceptible of contraction and expansion. Like water issuing out of the hole of a leather-bag, Consciousness streams through the avenues of the senses, and contacts objects. Contraction and Expansion are like the serpent and its coiling up. All Consciousness is essentially self-evident (or self-authoritative), and is self-luminous. The hypothetical[213] Consciousness is the means (or instrument) at one's disposal for all functions concerned with it, for such a function is made possible by it without seeking the aid of another thing *sui generis*, like object (*Artha*), sense (*Indriya*), Light (*Dīpa*), *etc.*[214]

[213] Referring to any other School which may admit no such thing as Consciousness. Problematical.

[214] Like light not requiring the aid of another light to be seen: one object another object; and sense, another sense.

No sameness of genus can be instituted as between Sight and Light; for the differentiation between (them) accrues from the variations imbedded in the Ahaṁkāric Taijasā Principles.[215]

By this (delineation given of Consciousness), the opinions, that (1) Consciousness is instantaneous, (2) it is endurant for three (successive or continuous) instants, (3) its illusory nature even in matters-of-fact (*Vyāvahārika*) transactions, as it is in matters phantasmal (*Prātibhāsika*),* (4) its nature demonstrable by other proof (i.e., not self-evident), (5) its being the Soul itself, *etc.*, are discarded. The Consciousness relating to (say): 'Pillar' (in the first instant) is the same one as that relating to 'Pillar' (in the succeeding instant), only it is continuous.[216]

---

[215] *Refer* to Advent IV for the explanation of these Principles or Material Categories.

* *I.E.*, The rope appearing, or illusorily striking one, as snake; or the deceptions or illusions of sense producing illusory Consciousness, i.e., knowledge hallucinatory;—or a mental hallucination.

[216] *Lit.*, the stream of Consciousness (*Dhārāvāhika-jñāna*). The Consciousness which is apprehensive of any object at one moment, is but its

'Granting that on the strength of Scriptures (Āgama), Consciousness is eternal, how are the conditions obtaining in the waking, sleeping *etc.*, states (of Consciousness) to be explained? The answer (to such a query) is: 'The burning quality of fire placed near a thing to be burnt is neutralised by the presence of a gem[217] etc; in like manner the presence of a certain hindering darkness produces sleep and other states. Also it is like (the state of) youth *etc.*, for, virility (the state of youth) is latent in (the age of) infancy, but becomes manifest in (the age of) youth.'[218]

Consciousness is of the character of attribute (*Guṇa*), by virtue of the definition that what is dependent (on another, in an indiscerptible

---

stream when the apprehension in the next moment is concerning the same object. Hence they are not two distinct Consciousnesses, the antecedent one dying, and the consequent one newly born as it were as the *Mādhyamikā* School of the Buddhists holds.

[217] It is believed there are some gems or stones and other substances which paralyse the power of fire to burn.

[218] *Consult* Vedānta-Sūtras: II. 3. 31:—"*Pumstvā*"-*divattvasya* &c."

manner) is its attribute (or quality), like the attributes (of substances).* Also by virtue of its (Consciousness's) susceptibility to contraction and expansion, it partakes of the character of substance (*Dravya.*) How Consciousness, the attribute of the Soul (*Ātma*), can be of the nature of substance, need not provoke doubt, for like the light, the same one substance can possess both the characteristics (of *attribute* and *substance*). Hence there is no contradiction.[219]

Substance (*Dravya*) is enunciable as that which is the abode (or seat) of states (*Avasthā*). Its radiation (or dispersion) outside its abode is possible like light (raying out from its centre). A syllogism (may be constructed) thus:—

Attributive Consciousness is Substance,
For it possesses the character of diffusion *etc.*,
Like light; or,
Consciousness is Substance,

---

* Like the "Blue Sky," where blueness is the inseparable adjunct of the sky.

[219] This contention is perhaps better understood if we say that Consciousness is the faculty as well as the function of the soul.

For, apart from its connection (or source) unseen, it is cognisable,[220]

Like Soul.

For Consciousness as stated, is conceivable as capable of simultaneously coming in contact with infinite space, like rays emerging from the eye, Sun *etc.* The terms synonymous with Consciousness are *Mati, Prajñā, Samvit, Dhishaṇā, Dhīḥ, Manīshā, Šemushī, Medhā, Buddhi, etc.* It is Consciousness which, affected by environment, assumes the forms of joy, grief, desire, hate, and will; for there are no means (or proof), justifying the assumption of a generating Cause of joy *etc.*, other than Consciousness. Like 'I remember' indicative of Consciousness, 'I desire,' 'I hate' (etc), indicate but a state of Consciousness. But how is the passage, which avers: 'Desire, will, doubt, zeal, indifference, courage, timidity, shame, sense (or reason) fear and all such, is Manas (mind),'[221] to be

---

[220] Take sun-light for example. The light is seen though its source the sun may remain unseen, or beyond the range of vision.

[221] [*Bṛhadâ-"raṇyaka Up. I.* 5. 3]:—"Kāmas-, saṅkalpa-, vicikitsā-, śraddhā-, (a) śraddhā-, dhṛtir-,

construed as signifying forms (or states) of consciousness? This query is met by the answer that inasmuch as the invariable law holds, associating mind (*Manas*) as the instrument (or internal sense) of Consciousness, the use of the term mind to signify Consciousness (as in the above passage) is figurative (-ly justified).

Likewise the qualities of the soul, which are numerous, are but the states of the attributive Consciousness, such (for example) as:—Perception, Inference, Word, Memory, Doubt, Conclusion, Difference, Fancy, Discernment, Endeavour, Temptation, Attachment, Hostility, Pride, Envy, Craving, Ostentation, Cupidity, Anger, Dignity, Stupor, Deceipt, Partiality,

---

adhṛtir-, hrīr-, dhīr-, bhīr-, etat sarvam mana eva." According to Occidental Philosophy, mind is immaterial and is a function of, or a spiritual force operating on, the brain; but in Oriental Philosophy, mind is the internal material organ of sense, the *Sense Commune*, and Consciousness is the attribute of soul that streams out to the objective world, by first passing through the aperture, so to say, of the mind, thence to the external senses and out thence to external objects.

Sorrow *etc*; and Wisdom, Folly, Love, Contentment, Discontent, Greatness, Fatigue, Fame, Renunciation, Enjoyment, Friendship, Compassion, Aspiration of Release (*mumukshā*), Bashfulness, Patience, Discrimination, Wish to Conquer, Softness, Forgival, Wish to do, Disgust, Imagination, Hypocrisy, Jealousy, Wish to kill, Cupidity, Vanity, Predilection, Prejudice, Dispute, (God-) Love (*bhakti*), Surrender (to God = *prapatti*), Lordship (or Power = Bhūti) *etc.*

Similarly the innumerable Blessed Attributes of God (*Bhagavān*) are the amplifications of His Consciousness and Power, such as:—Knowledge, Power, Strength, Glory, Might and Light, Freedom, Love, Gentleness, Rectitude, Friendliness, Impartiality, Compassion, Sweetness, Dignity, Magnanimity, Tactfulness, Patience, Courage, Valour, Bravery etc. Knowledge (*Jñāna*) is that (quality) which is of the nature of universal understanding. Power (*Šakti*) is the capability of causing existence from non-existence. Strength (*Bala*) is the capacity to endure. Glory (*Aišvarya*) is the capacity to rule. Might (*Vīrya*) is imperturbation. Light (*Tejas*) is the

14

power to resist. Freedom (*Sau-śilya*) is the capacity to mix freely with high and low. Love (*Vātsalya*) is the quality of finding good in evil, or the overlooking of fault. Gentleness (*Mārdava*) is the not bearing to be separated from one's dears. Rectitude (*Ārjava*) is to be straight in thought, word and deed. Friendliness (*Sauhārda*) is readiness to help others to the neglect of one's self. Impartiality (*Sāmya*) is to be equally accessible to all irrespective of their race, character or conduct. Compassion (*Kāruṇya*) is the wish to repair others' ills to one's own detriment, or the inability to see others' sufferings. Sweetness (*Mādhurya*) is to be sweet while nourishing, like milk. Dignity (*Gāmbhīrya*) is the power which forbids the inquiry for deep motives underlying such acts as conferring abundance *etc.*, on the devotees. Magnanimity (*Audārya*) is the feeling of dissatisfaction even after bestowing plenty. Tactfulness (*Cāturya*) is the power to hide another's faults. Patience (*Sthairya*) is to be unruffled. Courage (*Dhairya*) is the power of permitting no waver, after decision.

Valour (*Śaurya*) is the power to rush into the midst of the enemy; Bravery (*Parākrama*) is gaining victory over him. The others (attributes) may be similarly understood.

The nature of God-love (*bhakti*)[222] and God-surrender (*Prapatti*)[222]—states of Consciousness—will briefly be discussed (now). It is God alone who confers Moksha (Final Release from material existence), on the (bare) plea (furnished by souls) of Love and Surrender. Hence these (latter) are considered as the Means to Release. The character of Means assigned also to *Karmayoga*[223] and *Jñāna-yoga*,[223] which in fact are inseparable from Love, is by reason of (such) predominant characteristics persons may severally (happen to) possess.[224]

---

[222] *Bhakti* is Love or Welling Emotion to God; *Prapatti* is Surrender or Dedication to God (Faith).

[223] *Karma* = Reaching Salvation by means of good acts; *Jñāna*, by means of meditation (thought). See the Subject enlarged: Pp. 581 *ff*. JRAS. for July, 1910. Also see *infra*.

[224] This means that in some persons, the active quality may be more manifest, in others thought or intellect more predominant; and yet the consummation of them all are to be found in Love.

What is *Karma-Yoga* or the Path of Works? Through Holy Teaching (got), one acquires true knowledge regarding Soul and God; and, according to his best ability performs, without regard for fruit, diverse actions of virtue:—*Kāmya* or Optional, *Nitya* or Routine, and *Naimittika* or Casual. The sum of acts so done is *Karma-Yoga*. It branches itself into God-worship, Austerities, Resort to Holy Places, Charity, Sacrifices *etc*. Effecting the riddance of stains on the soul, it engenders *Jñāna-Yoga* or the Path of Knowledge, and through it or direct, engenders *Bhakti-Yoga* or the Path of Love.[224]

What is *Jñāna-Yoga* or the Path of Knowledge? By means of *Karma-Yoga*, one's heart (or mind, *antah-karaṇa*) becomes purified, and he then contemplates on the Soul which is distinct from matter, and liege to God. This (contemplation or *Jñāna-Yoga*) is useful to Love (*Bhakti*.) Whether these Ways (or Paths) are Independent Means (to Salvation), or ancillary

---

[224] Read Pp. 581 *ff*. *Artha-Pañcaka*, JRAS. for July, 1910. Also the Soteriological Table in (my) *Bhagavad-Gītā*, Pp. 573-574.

to Love, depend upon the several authorities presenting such views.

What is *Bhakti-Yoga* or the Path of Love? It is an unbroken stream of thought (of God) like a stream of (poured) oil, preceded by the eight-fold auxiliaries: *Yama*, *Niyama* (moral and physical restraints), *Āsana* (postures), *Prāṇâ"yāma* (restraint of breath), *Pratyâ"hāra* (restraint of senses), *Dhāraṇa* (steadying concentration), *Dhyāna* (uninterrupted meditation), *Samādhi* (imperturbable fixture).*

The seven-fold means known as (1) *Viveka*, (2) *Vimoka*, (3) *Abhyāsa*, (4) *Kriyā*, (5) *Kalyāṇa*, (6) *Anavasāda* and *Anuddharsha*, give birth to it (*Bhakti*). Of these, (1) *Viveka* or Discrimination is said to be the purity of body effected by abstention from food, impure from any cause. (2) *Vimoka* or Dispassion is freedom from desire. (3) *Abhyāsa* or Practice is the repeated habit of clinging to the (mental) Subject (or Image) (of contemplation). (4) *Kriyā* or Performance is the observance of the Fivefold

---

* The last three terms may perhaps be better translated by Abstraction, Devotion and Exaltation.

Mahā-Yajñas or Great Sacrifices,[225] according to one's ability. (5) *Kalyāṇa* or Virtues are Truth, Uprightness, Clemency, Non-cruelty and Non-cupidity. (6) *Anavasāda* or Painlessness is freedom from dejection (or despair). (7) *Anuddharsha* or Non-elation is freedom from paroxysmal joy; for such joy is also a hindrance. Fostered thus by this seven-fold Means, Love (*Bhakti*) becomes as vivid as actual perception and (this) must last till the (final) dissolution of the body occurs. This final (God-) consciousness may break (on a person) at the *finis* of this or some other body.

Love or *Bhakti,* variously called *Vedana, Dhyāna* and *Upāsana,* has three successive stages, (1) *Para-bhakti,* (2) *Para-jñāna* and (3) *Parama-bhakti.*[226] Love again is twofold:

---

[225] *Vide* 'Taittirīya Araṇyaka' 3:—"*Deva-yajñaḥ Pitṛ-yajño, Bhūta-yajño, Manushya-yajño, Brahma-yajña,* iti." I. E. Sacrifices to the Gods, the Manes, Creatures, Men and God.

[226] Read the verse: "*Darśanam* (1) *para-bhaktis-syāt, Para-jñānaṁtu* (2) *saṅgamam, punar viśleshа-bhīrutvam Paramā-bhaktir* (3) *uccyate.*" (1) Seeing God, (2) Uniting with God, and (3) Fear of separation from Him.

Sādhana-bhakti or Laboured Love, and *Phala-bhakti* or Ripened Love. Laboured Love is what is evoked by (human) exertion. Ripened Love is what is gifted by God's grace, such that is found in Parāṅkuśa, Nātha[227] *etc.* The employment of the term 'love' for praise, prostration *etc.*, alluded to in such verses as:

'Love of My votaries,' *etc*[228].,

is tropical.

But a query may arise why, when the Vedāntas have prescribed Hearing (*Śravaṇa*) and Reflection (*Manana*) also, love (*Bhakti* or *Nididhyāsana*) alone is said to be enjoined. It is met thus: A person having learnt (the letter of) the Vedas with all its adjuncts, finds that the import of all this (learning) must have some definite motive; he necessarily resorts to Hearing (i. e. exposition by a Teacher) in order

---

[227] Parāṅkuśa or St. Nammâzhvār typifies all the Saints or Āzhvārs, and Nātha-muni, all the Sages or Ācāryas.

[228] *Mad-bhakta-jana-vātsalyam, pūjāyāñ câ"numo-danam......bhaktir ashṭa-vidhāhy eshā'* etc, [Vishṇu-dharmottara; quoted in Course V. Prapanna-Pārijāta also].

to ascertain for himself what it (the end) may be. Hence Hearing as a necessary step is premised. Reflection then (on what was taught) is also premised inasmuch as it is a (mental) process intended to render steady what has been heard.* Hence there is no inconsistency when it is averred that the purpose (of the Vedas) is to prescribe Love (*Bhakti*). Love which in other words is meditation (*Dhyāna*), becomes manifold by the diversity of its Methods (*Vidyā*). These Methods (of Love or Meditation) are subsumable under two main heads: (1) those that have for their fruit (aim) Material Goods, or Spiritual End (*Mukti*). The Udgīta-Vidyā *etc.*, belong to the Material Class. Those that belong to the Spiritual Class or the Brahma-Vidyā, are such as the Antar-akshi-Vidyā, Antarâ-'ditya-Vidyā, Dahara-Vidyā, Bhūma-Vidyā, Sad-Vidyā, Madhu-Vidyā, Upakosala-Vidyā, Śāṇḍilya-Vidyā, Purusha-Vidyā, Pratardana-Vidyā,

* This is with reference to the Text: *Ātmā vâ 're-drashṭavyas' śrotavyo mantavyaḥ* &c.' [Bṛhad-Āraṇ: Up. II. 4. 5]. And also read: "*Sthāṇurayam bhāra-hāraḥ kilā'bhūt adhītya Vedam navijānāti yo'rtham.*" [Commy; to III, Saṁhit-opanishad-Brāhmaṇa].

Vaiśvānara-Vidyā, Pañca-'gni-Vidyā *etc.* [229] Nyāsa-Vidyā[230] is *Prapatti* or Surrender (to God). It is the same as *Śaraṇā-gati* or Capitulation (to God) as the Refuge (or harbour), as defined in the Verse:—

'Prapatti or Śaraṇāgati is imploring, with abounding love, God alone as the Way for consummation of aspirations otherwise unattainable' [231]

This (Way,) which guarantees the Spiritual End (*Moksha*) at the end of the present body, precludes the necessity of the state of being (vividly) conscious of God at the time of death,* requires but once to be done, is designated *Nyāsa* (lying or leaning on God), *Śaraṇāgati* (He

---

[229] Consult the Table of the *Vidyās* in my *Bhagavad-Gītā.* Pp. 129-130.

[230] No. 32 in this Table.

[231] 'Ananya-sādhye svābhishṭe
Mahā-viśvāsa-pūrvakam.
Tad-ek--opāyatā yācñā,
Prapattiś śaraṇâgatiḥ [*Ahirbudhnya-Saṁhitā,* Pāñcarātra].

* Read: '*Aśaktam api ca smartum ante pūrva-kṛtam smaran, svayam eva Param Dhāma svayam nayati Mādhavaḥ* [Bhāradvāja-Saṁhitā, IV. 80]'

the only Refuge). It is thus a unique state of consciousness. Further descant on this topic is debarred by reason of this work having been designed for the enlightenment of the young; it has to be learnt from the properly constituted apostolic authorities, out of esoteric treatises (*Rahasyas*) *etc.*

As only Love (*bhakti*) and Surrender (*prapatti*) are admittted as the Means by which to secure the Spiritual Consummation (*Moksha*), Means that others promulgate are discarded. Amongst those (religionists) who stand outside the pale of the Vedas, some do not admit the entity Soul at all, as apart from the body; to them the very subject of Deliverance (*Moksha*) is futile.[232] Nor is it less abortive to those others who believe consciousness to be momentary, which to them is itself the Soul.[233] But they may contend that it (Deliverance) may be predicated for the next begotten consciousness. But it cannot be that one (lapsed thing) can exert

[232] The Materialists, Hedonists, *Cārvākas* or *Lokāyatikas.*

[233] The Buddhist *Mādhyamikas.*

for another (*for Moksha*).[234] Nor for those can the question (of Deliverance) arise, who are addicted to the many-faced *sapta-bhaṅgi* profession.[235] Nor can there be partisans for the school of the Vaiśeshikas who assert the Spiritual End (or Deliverance) to be petrifaction (*Pāshāṇa-kalpa*). Nor is the subject (Deliverance) of any value to the Sāṅkhyas, who do not admit God (*Īśvara*), and there arises a doubt as to whom is Deliverance, Soul (*Purusha*) or to Matter (*Prakṛti*)? Nor is that question invested with interest for those schoolmen, the illusionists,[236] to whom the true

[234] That is, if each Consciousness (which itself is Soul), is momentarily anew, it is absurd to speak of *moksha* for which one prior consciousness prepares the way for another as both of them are independent and unconnected by continuity.

[235] The Jainas who hold the System of the Seven Paralogisms: (1) 'may be, it is,' (2) 'may be, it is not,' (3) 'may be, it is and is not, (4) 'may be, is not predicable,' (5) 'may be, is and not predicable, (6) 'may be, is not and not predicable'. (7) 'may be, is and is not and not predicable.' [*Vide, Sarva-darśana-saṁgraha* by Mādhava].

[236] The *Māyāvadins* or *Advaitins* of the Vedānta School.

monic knowledge cannot spring from the avowed illusory nature of the (Vedic) texts. The contention of (the Schools of) Bhaskara and Yādava for a combined Way of Works *cum* Knowledge, is likewise inadmissible. The Śaiva system is discarded by reason of its averring Paśupati as the Goal, and the smearing of ashes *etc*,—contrary to the spirit of the Vedas,—as the Means.[287]

Thus consciousness has been expounded.

Thus ends Advent VII,
The Treatment of Attributive Consciousness
(*Dharma-bhūta-jñāna*)
in the
"Light of the School of Rāmānuja."

---

[287] See this System refuted by all the Three Ācāryas, Śaṅkarā, Rāmānuja and Madhva, in the Vedānta-Sūtras: *Patyur asāmañjas syāt* [II. 2. 35] and elsewhere. That Rāmānuja based his Commentaries on Brahma-sūtras on Śrīkaṇṭha's model, as is supposed by later Śaiva Schools is refuted by Appaya-Dīkshita (a Śaiva himself) in his work, *Śivârka-maṇi-dīpikā*. Vallabha in his *Aṇu-bhāshya* accuses Śaivâcaryas of plagiarism from Rāmānuja [Pp: 48 and 1403 *passim*].

ADVENT VIII.

THE SOUL (*Jiva*).

The (category) Soul or Jīva will now be explained. The characteristics common to Soul and God are: Interiority (*pratyaktva*), Cognoscitiveness (*cetanatva*), Spiritness (*ātmatva*), and Agency (*kartṛtva*).

Pratyaktva or Interiority means to be self-luminous. *Cetanatva* or Cognoscitiveness is to be the seat (or involucre) of consciousness. *Ātmatva* or Spiritness is to be the antithesis to body (matter). *Kartṛtva* or Agency is to be the seat of consciousness, of the form of Will (*saṅkalpa*).

Having thus stated the common characteristics of Soul, the special (or singular) characteristics will now be stated. Atomic *cum* Cognoscitive, Liegent *cum* Cognoscitive; similarly, Sustained, Contingent, Agent by delegation, Subject, and so forth; may be conceived (as qualities distinguishing the Soul).

The Soul is distinct from body, senses, mind (*manas*), breath, and intellect. Distinct from body (Soul is) by reason of the experience: '*My* body'; Distinct from the outer senses by reason of the experiences: 'I see with (*my*) eyes', 'I hear with (*my*) sense of hearing', 'I speak with *my* tongue' and so forth; Distinct from mind (*manas*) as this is known to be a sense; from breath as indicated by the expression: '*My* breath', and from Intellect (*buddhi*) as borne out by the experience: '*I* know'. It is atomic (or monadic) by reason of the *Šruti* (=Scriptures) stating that it (Soul) out-goes (from the body at time of leaving, and in-comes to the body at time of joining), confirmed by (our own) experience. No question need arise how, if Soul is atomic, it is capable of cognising simultaneously many objects, for (its) attributive consciousness has the capacity for such diffusion.[288] By this (law), the

[288] 'Atomic' has a material significance which is not meant, as the Soul, is spiritual. What is intended to be conveyed is that Soul is a subtle spiritual centre of consciousness, a focus of the forces of consciousness which can ray out anywhere, like the central sun diffusing its rays anywhere. 'A spiritual

assumption of many bodies (simultaneously) by such (sages) as Saubhari,[239] and by the Freed (*Muktas*) becomes possible. This (Soul) is Eternal, for it remembers what was experienced in the past. But it may be asked: how if Soul is eternal, they do speak of its being 'born' and 'dead'? We reply that birth is because of the Soul's bondage with body, and death is, because of its severance therefrom. Hence the nature of the Soul is Eternal. It is distinct for each distinct body. In a similar manner as the singular of the expression 'gold jar' is made use of for an 'aggregate' of gold jars, all of the same dimensions, and 'grain' is used for an accumulation of grains, is the (generic) term Soul used, as all souls share in common the attribute of consciousness. Hence there is no identity, as that conflicts with the Authorities.[240]

---

nucleolus of cognoscitive forces is Soul' would be an appropriate definition.

[239] See *Vishṇu-Purāṇa* [IV-2] for the story.

[240] This is with reference to the *advaitic* (monistic) theory that all souls are identical; whereas Authorities such as the Vedas mean otherwise, i.e. assert plurality or multiplicity of souls.

It is by nature Blissful (or essentially Joyous); but, infected by environment (*upādhi*), falls into migration (*samsāra*). It is Agent (*kartā*), enjoyer (*bhoktā*), the Bodied (*śarīrī*) and body (*śarīra*). It is the bodied with reference to matter; with reference to God (*Īśvara*), it is body.

That it is Self-luminous (*svayam-prakāśa*) is evident from Perception as well as Word (Scriptures). A syllogism may be constructed as follows:—

'The Soul is Self-luminous.'

For it is conscious, (or cognoscitive).

Like the attributive consciousness.'

Consciousness-ness (*jñānatva*) and Stainlessness (or Sinlessness *amalatva*) *etc.*, are qualities which determine its (Soul's) Essence.

Thus the thesis of the Bauddhas that as consciousness is momentary, Soul is the concatenation of (such) moments;—the thesis of the Cārvākas that Soul is conterminous with the body, which is a compound of Four Elements;—the thesis of the Jainas that Soul is commensurate with the elephant's body in the elephant, and commensurate with the ant's body in the ant ;—the thesis of Yādava that Soul is a fragment of God (*Brahman*);—the thesis of Bhāskara that Soul is a division of the conditioned God (*Brahman*);—the thesis that Soul is a fabrication (effected) by nescience ;—the thesis that Soul is multipled by reason of the limiting (or circumscribing) Inner Organ (*Antaḥkaraṇa*) ; all other such objectionable theses are disannulled ; and likewise the contention for its (Soul's) infinitive nature (*vibhutva*).

But if it be asked, how, in case of not admitting the infinitive character of Soul, is its fruit in connection with other realms, determined by the 'unseen' (destiny = *adṛsha*), possible, the reply is that though Soul has no local (or spatial) relation, yet the Unseen (destiny) determines it. What is Destiny? It is a species of consciousness attained as a consequence of good deeds done for winning the pleasure of God (*Bhagavān*). This consciousness is none other than Providence (or Will) of God, contingent on His infinitive (*vibhu*) nature.*

* The purport of this is that it is God's providence that watches our behaviour, and rewards us. See Vedānṭa-Sūtras ; '*Phalam ata upapatteḥ*' [III. 2, 37.]

(In) thus (predicating) the reaping of fruit (by the Soul), is not beset with difficulties.

This Soul is threefold: Bound (*Baddha*), Freed (*Mukta*), and Free or Eternal (*Nitya*). Of these the Bound are those particular group of souls, from Brahmā down to the worm, inhabiting the fourteen worlds comprising the 'Oval Sphere.' Brahmā is sprung from the navel-lotus of Śrīman-Nārāyaṇa; Rudra from Brahmā; from Brahmā again are sprung the Yogis Sanaka *etc.*, the Devarshis Nārada *etc.*, the Brahmarshis Vasishṭha *etc.*, the Nine Prajāpatis, Pulastya, Marīci, Daksha, Kaśyapa *etc.* From these sprang the Devas, the Regents of the Quarters (*Dik-pālakas*), the Fourteen Indras, the Fourteen Manus, the Asuras, Pitṛs, Siddhas, Gandharvas, Kinnaras, Kimpurushas, Vidyādharas *etc.*, the Vasus, Rudras, Ādityas, the Aśvinis, and the Dānavas, Yakshas, Rākshasas Piśācas, Guhyakas *etc.* Thus there are many varieties of creatures of Deva-Origin. The human class also has many varieties such as Brāhmaṇas, Kshatriyas, Vaiśyas, Sūdras *etc.* So also is the animal species such as cattle, beasts, birds, reptiles, moths, worms *etc.* The stationary* class is also diverse such as trees, bushes, creepers, shrubs, grasses *etc.* Trees *etc.*, possess sufficient consciousness (intelligence), necessary to imbibe water *etc.*, as evident from the text :—

"That (consciousness) is meagre in the lowest forms of life".[241]

Thus the Bound (*Baddha* souls) are of the classes: Devas (celestial or superhuman), human, animal and stationary.*

These are again (differently) classifiable as womb-born, egg-born, seed-born and sweat-born. The Devas and man are womb-born, (but) among them Brahmā, Rudra *etc.*, Sanaka *etc.*, Sītā, Draupadī, Dṛshṭadyumna *etc.*, are not thus born (*ayonija*), so are the Bhūtas, Bhetāḷas *etc.* The animals *etc.*, are (some) womb-born, (some) egg-born, and (some) sweat-born. The Stationary *etc*, are seed-born.[242] The Bound (souls), thus delineated, are constantly

---

[241] '*Aprāṇa vatsu svalpā sā sthāvareshu tato 'dhikā*' [Vishṇu-Purāṇa ; VI. 7. 64] Also *Cf.* with *Manu-Smṛti* I. 49 "*Antas-saṁjñā bhavanty etc* &c ".

* Stationary = Vegetable and Mineral Kingdoms.

[242] Read *Manu-Smṛti* : I., verses 5 to 50.

whirled in the (material) wheel, fashioned from (the elements of) *Avidyā* (nescience), *Karma* (acts), *Vāsana* (predispositions), *Ruci* (craving) and association with matter, meandering like a stream with neither beginning nor end, or like the never-ending process of 'seed and plant';[243] subject to the chequered conditions (or plights) (of life known as) gestation, birth, infancy, youth; waking, dream, sleep, trance, dotage, death; heaven (*svarga*), hell, *etc.*; suffering terribly in untold ways the three kinds of afflictions;[244] and forfeiting the estate of God-bliss,—their rightful heritage.

These (souls again) are of two classes: (1) Subject to Śāstra, and (2) Non-subject to Śāstra. Among these, liability to Śāstra pertain to those Bound (souls) who have the (moral) consciousness dependant on the several senses. Such is not the case with animals and stationary (creatures). The (souls) subject to Śāstra are of two classes (again): coveters of material

---

[243] *Bīja-vṛksha-nyāya*; i. e. the never-ending recurrence of plant from seed, and seed from plant.

[244] The *ādhyātmika*, self-inflicted: *ādhibhautika*, other-inflicted; *ādhidaivikā*, by divine visitation.

happiness (*bubhukshu*) and coveters of spiritual happiness (*mumukshu*). The former cling to the Triad[245] of life-ambitions. These (again) are of two classes: those that cling to Wealth and Delights, and those that cling to Duty. The former are those who labour under the notion that body is soul. The latter are those who are launched on Sacrifices (*yajña*), Charity (*dāna*), Austerities (*tapas*), Pilgrimage (*tīrtha-yātrā*) *etc.*, all falling under the head 'Duty' as per the enunciation:—

'Duty is that which paves the way for happiness to come (*alaukika*)' and,

'Duty is that which is the Way (or means), established by (incentive) Injunction.'[246]

---

[245] The four ambitions of life are: (1) *Dharma* (duty) (2) *artha* (wealth) (3) *kāma* (delights) and (4) *moksha* (redemption). (1), (2) and (3) constitute the Triad, called *Traivargika*, and (4) is the *Apavarga*.

[246] [Jaimini-Sūtras; I. 1. 2]; '*Codanā-lakshaṇoiya 'rtho dharmah.*' i.e., the injunctions of the Scriptures (*alaukika*) alone *provide* the incentive to duty, which done, does not bring to the man immediate result as would accrue to a worldly effort on which an immediately realisable corresponding fruit is always contingent.

These are believers in the Soul as distinct from the body, and in that there is the other (highest or spiritual) world to come. The partisans of Duty (*dharma*) are of two classes (again): those, adherents of other deities; and those, of God (*Bhagavān*). The adherents of other deities are the worshippers of Brahmā, Rudra *etc.* The adherents of God are those devotees who come under the text:

'The aggrieved, the seeker, the ambitious &c.'[247]

The aggrieved (*ārta*) is he who has lost his fortune and is desirous of recovering it. The ambitious (*arthārthi*) is he who longs to grow rich anew. The Seekers (of redemption, *Mumukshu*) are of two classes, viz., those who wish for Isolation (*kaivalya*) and those who wish for Divinity (*moksha*). *Kaivalya* or Isolation is the meta-physical soul-bliss secured by the Path of Knowledge (*jñāna*). This Soul-bliss is isolate from God-bliss, and is experienced in a Corner of the Spiritual Universe,—in the manner

---

[247] *Ārto, jigñāsur, arthārthī, jñānī, ca Bharatarshabha* | &c. [Bhagavad-Gītā: VII. 16].

of the wife who has lost her husband,—after travelling along the Way of Light *etc.* (*arcir-ādi-mārga*).[248] Some opine that as those who have travelled along the Path of Light can no more return, there is a Corner assigned in the Physical Universe itself, where they are absorbed in their own Soul-bliss (*ātmâ-'nubhava*).

The Aspirers for Divinity or God-bliss are of two kinds: (1) The God-lovers (*bhaktas*), and (2) the God-leaners (*prapannas*). The God-lovers are those who have learnt the Vedas with all its limbs and the Upanishads (*śiraska*), become versed in the metaphysics of the Vedas, early and later parts thereof, thereby acquiring the Knowledge of God (*Brahman*), as Him who is distinct from (the Categories) of Conscients (*cit*) and Non-conscients (*acit*),—as Him whose essential nature is bliss, exalted and measureless,—as Him who is hostile to all evil and full of all Holy Graces; and then resort to the Path of Love (*bhakti*) leading to Him, thereby aspiring to reach salvation (*moksha*).

---

[248] Read *Bhagavad-Gītā*: VIII. 24 *ff* and analogous Upanishadic passages.

The fitness for (the Path of) Love abide in the Vārṇic Triad[249], as also in the Devas (deities or superhuman creatures); for in these the attitude of supplication (*arthitva*), and ability to perform (*bhakti*) (*sāmarthya*), subsist.[249b]. The Śūdras are not entitled thereto, for reasons argued out in the *Apa-śūdra* Section.[250]

The Character of (God-) Love has been delineated in the Section on Consciousness (VII). The (God-)Lovers are of two kinds: (1) those who practise love with a Motive (*sādhana*), and (2) those who practise the same as an End in itself (*sādhya*). Vyāsa *etc*, belong to the former class; Nātha (muni) *etc*, to the latter.

The Surrendered (*prapanna*, or God-Leaner) is he who is distinguished by the qualifications of

---

[249] *I. e.*, the Three Empowered or Eligible Classes or Castes (*Varṇa*), viz. Brāhmaṇa, Kshatriya and Vaiśya.

[249b] See Vedānta-Sūtras: [I. 3. 25]; '*Tad upary api Bādarāyaṇas sambhavāt.*' Also Cp. with Ṛk-Samhitā, X. 167-1; '*Indra!......tapaḥ paritapy ājayasva*'.

[250] Vedānta-Sūtras: [I. 3. 33]; *Śug asya tad-anādara-'śravaṇāt*' etc.

Waylessness and *Resortlessness*;[281] and reposes (solely) on the Lord (*Bhagavān*). He (or It) is of two sorts: who longs for the Triad of objects,[282] and who longs for emancipation (*moksha*). The aspirer for the Triad is he who longs for the fulfilments of duty, for wealth and for joys.[283] The aspirer for emancipation (or the Supreme Goal) is he who by association with the good (and wise) has acquired discrimination of what is lasting and what fleeting, what transcendent and what insignificant, and thereby loses all relish (*vairāgya*) for worldliness (*samsāra*) and pants for salvation (*moksha*). To attain this desired end he repairs to a Spiritual Teacher (*ācārya*), who is indued with adequate qualities as per text:—

'The Teacher is the versed in the Vedas etc';[283]

---

[281] See a Treatise on these two qualifications by Piḷḷai Lokācārya, Englished in the *Indian Antiquary* for November, 1910. 'He' used for Soul is same as 'It'.

[282] I. e. *Dharma, Artha, Kāma* (the *Traivargika*.) See note 245, p: 125.

[283] *Ācāryo Veda-sampannaḥ Vishṇu-bhakto vimatsaraḥ mantrajño mantra-bhaktaś ca sadā mantrāśrayaś śuciḥ.* [Dvay-opanishat].

and through him seeks Śrī the (Saviour), in Whom vests the function of mediation (*purusha-kāra*)* and (finally), realising his lack of power to pursue the Paths of Love *etc.*, and therefore realising his position as one who is bereft of all Ways and Means (*akiñ-cano-(a)nanya-gatiḥ*) † accepts as his sole Means of salvation, the Holy Feet of the Blessed Lord (*Srīman-Nārāyaṇa*). Such is the God-leaner (*prapanna*).

Surrender (*prapatti*) is the High Path to all. The surrendered (God-leaner) is of two sorts: the One-pointed (*Ekānti*) and the One-only-pointed (*Param-aikānti*). The One-Pointed is the person who addresses himself to God alone for the grant of other (i.e. worldly) boons as well as salvation (*moksha*); and is therefore one to whom other deities (or demi-gods) are of no account. The One-only-pointed is the person who does not crave for any boons even from God Himself except

* See note 3.

† See Piḷḷai Lokâ'cārya's *Rahasya*: 'The Refugee's Refuge' in the 'Indian Antiquary,' Vol. xxxix, November, 1910.

Knowledge and Love (of Him).[254] This latter is again of two sorts: the Patient and the Impatient. The Patient is he who bows to the inevitable suffering-out of the fructescent (*prārabdha*) karma, according to the text:—

'Inevitably it must be suffered *etc.*,'[255] and (patiently) waits for salvation to follow on the expiry of (the term of) this body. The Impatient is he who feels his presence in worldliness unbearable, as if he were placed in the midst of raging flames, and pants for deliverance (or redemption) immediately on craving God therefor.

The Freed (*mukta* or the Absolved) is he who has accepted the Path, and performs all duties: routine, casual, and all decrees of the Divine, primary and secondary, for the sake of duty. He avoids all offences against God and the Godly; and at the time of casting off the body,

[254] Read: '*Tat-pāda-bhakti-jñānābhyām phalam anyat kadācana, na yācet praṇato Vishṇum yācanān naśyati dhruvam.*'

[255] '*Avaśyam anubhokṭavyam kṛtam karma śubhâ-'śubham, nâ 'bhuktam kshīyate karma kalpa-koṭi śatair api*'. [Mahā-Bhārata ?].

bequeaths his merits and demerits to his friends and foes (respectively); * and rests in peace in the Supreme Lord who abideth in the heart, as stated in the text:—

'Rest speech in mind *etc.*'[286]

(After resting thus a while), It (the Soul) enters into the organ (called the) *Sushumnā*, the door to the Spiritual State (*mukti*), and thence emerges out of the (head-) Orifice (called the) *Brahma-randhra*. Accompanied by the Lord (abiding) in the heart, It thence passes along the rays of the Sun to the world of Fire (*agni-loka*), and thence journeys on, adored on the Way by the Presiding Deities of the Day, the Half-month, the Summer Solstice, the Year *etc*, and (the Deity) Air. From there It speeds through the sphere of the Sun, and through the wheel of his chariot and the stars, enters the world of the Sun. Thence again It is conducted in great ceremony by the Hosts of Guides

---

* For the distribution made of merits and demerits, see *Kaushītaki-Brāhmaṇ-opanishat*.

[286] [*Kaṭhopanishat* III. 13]: 'Yacched vāṅ manasi *prājñaḥ* etc.

(*ātivāhika*), the Moon, the Lightning (-Lord), Varuṇa, Indra, Prajāpati, *etc.* Passing thus through the several realms owned by these, It crosses (the River) Virajā, the boundary dividing matter from Vaikuṇṭha.* Here It casts off the subtle body, and is received by Amānava. It (the Soul) is now robed in an immaterial divine Form, four-armed, and is decorated Brahman-fashion. It (now) enters the City of Vaikuṇṭha,* with the permission of the sentinels bearing the names Indra and Prajāpati.[267] Passing through a towerd gate flying with banners and flanked by stretching ramparts, It feasts its eyes with the nectar-lake the Airammada, and the *ficus* tree the Soma-savana. It is now greeted by five hundred damsels, in groups of hundred, as stated in the text:—

'A hundred (damsels) with garlands in hand *etc*,'[267] and is beautified by Brahma-perfume

---

* The Heaven of heavens, or that Spiritual State which is delvered of all hindrances or limitations. See further, foot-note 2, to page 574, *Artha-Pañcaka*, JRAS, for July, 1910.

[267] See *Kaushitaki-Brāhmaṇ-opanishat*; as also *Chāndogya* and *Bṛhad-āraṇya*-Up° for all the descriptions

etc. It then salutes (the Eternals or Archangels) Ananta, Garuḍa, Vishvaksena *etc*, resident there and is equally treated so in return. It then proceeds to the Superb-gemmed Pavilion, and renders obeisance, at the (blessed) Seat, to Its Spiritual Teachers (who are there). Now It (Soul) approaches nearer the (Divine) Seat, where It finds the throne thereon, Dharma (*etc*).,-made, the Lotus over it, and Ananta over again. On the sides stand Vimalā *etc*, with fans (waving) in their hands, serving God (*Bhagavān*); Who is installed there with His (Queens) Śrī, Bhū and Nīḷā;-Who is bedecked with the Divine Weapons: Conch, Discus *etc.*;-Who is blazing with the countless Divine Ornaments, the Crown, the Diadem; and, for the head, ears, neck, breast, arms, wrists, waist and ankles, such (jewels) as Cūdāvataṁsa, Makarakuṇḍala, Graiveyaka-hāra, Keyūra, Kaṭaka, Śrīvatsa, Kaustubha, Muktā-damodara-bandhana, Pītāmbara, Kāñcīguṇa, Nūpura *etc*;[358]-and Who

---

here given of the Heavenly Sphere and the Heavenly Journey: also *Muṇḍak-opanishat.*

[358] Consult *Pāñcarātra* works for these details. The idea of the Personal God is here seen emphasis-

is the boundless Ocean of Graces. God so installed, the Soul sees; and approaching, plants Its foot on the Seat and is received into the lap of the Lord. To the inquiry 'Who art thou', Soul says, 'I am Thy-make', and His benign looks are dowered on It. From the ineffable bliss ensuant on joying with the Lord, Soul is lovingly stablished in Service to Him, at all places and for all times, in all situations and for all varieties (of service). The Octuple Graces[259] dawn on the Soul, and It is for ever more installed in the joy of the Lord (*Brahm-ānubhava*). Such Soul is the Absolved (*mukta*). Its equality with the Lord (*Brahman*) is as respects the bliss alone thereof[260]; for all concern with kosmic functions

---

ed to an extent satisfying as well the sage as the boor, and covers the whole scale of God's Being lying between the most absolute Ideal and the most concrete Symbol. For symbological explanations, see (my) *Lives of Saints*.

[259] See *Chāndogy-opanishat* VIII. 1. 5: '(1) *Apahata-pāpmā*, (2) *vijaro*, (3) *vimṛtyur*, (4) *viśoko* (5) *vijighatso*, (6) (a)-*pipāsas*, (7) *satya-kāmas*, (8) *satya-saṁkalpaḥ*.

[260] See Vedânta-Sūtras. IV. 4. 21: '*Bhoga-mātra-sāmya-lingāc ca*; See *Muṇḍak-opanishat*: III. 1. 3.

is precluded by hypothesis.[261] It could assume any form and visit any part of the Universe (at will). But if it be asked how, if the Absolved (*mukta*) returns not, as it is said,[262] It can be free to roam there, we say: Not so, the return precluded is that (entailed) by *karma*; not excursions at Its own (freed) will (and pleasure). Hence the Absolved Soul, ever in harmony with the Will of the Lord (*Bhagavān*), freely everywhere tours.

The Eternals (*Nityas* or the Ever-Free), are those whose function is never at variance with the Will of the Lord (*Bhagavān*), and never therefore are they subject to their consciousness (ever) becoming dimmed. They are Ananta, Garuḍa, Vishvaksena and others. The functions appointed them in perpetuity are determined by the Eternal Will of God. Their Incarnations, like the Incarnations of God Himself, are determined by choice (i. e. not compelled by *karma*).

In the manner aforesaid, the (Category of) Soul, comprised of the varieties of bound

---

[261] See *Ibid* IV. 4. 17: '*Jagad-vyāpāra-varjam* etc.

[262] See *Ibid*: [V. 4. 22]: '*Anāvṛttiś śabdāt* etc.

(*baddha*), freed (*mukta*), and eternal (*nitya*), has been depicted."[268]

Thus ends Advent VIII,
The Treatment of the Soul (*Jīva*)
in the
Light of the School of Rāmānuja.

***

---

[268] Read *Artha-pañcaka*, Pp: 572, JRAS, for July, 1910. If *svarga*, the Material paradise be translated as heaven, *Vaikuṇṭha*, the Spiritual Heaven becomes the Heaven of heavens. In all religions, the portrayal of this blessed state is necessarily made in material language. The saints of Christianity are, for example, said to be crowned with palms and amaranths, and perpetually singing hallelujas to God. Metaphorical language is thus unavoidable; but this is certain that whether such language be of the conventional type germane to the genius of the European or of the Asiatic, the idea of the blessed state is never of the sensual but of the spiritual, quite a different order therefore of existence. For a dissertation on this subject, which oft embarasses mankind, see *Introductions*, to (my) *Lives of Saints*, page xi *passim*.

ADVENT IX.

GOD (*Īśvara*).

Now (the category of) God (*Īśvara*) will be inquired into. The characteristics of God are All-Lordship, All-Mastership, All-worshipfulness by work, All-fruit-givership, All-Support, All-energising, All-Word-indicated, All-knowledge-goal, All-bodiedness excepting His own body and consciousness.*

God thus indicated is the Material (or Formal) Cause of the Universe by virtue of His aspect as the constituted of the Conscients and Non-conscients (*cid-acid-viśishṭaḥ*); is the Efficient (or Spiritual) Cause by virtue of His aspect as the Willer; and is the Instrumental Cause by virtue of His immanence in Time *etc*. The Material Cause is that which results as Effect by undergoing modification. The Efficient Cause is that

* The epigrammatic style here employed, is, it is hoped, sufficiently lucid. It at any rate obviates the nesessity for otherwise long-phrasing, detracting from the poetry attaching to terseness.

which causes modifications so as to result into Effect. The Instrumental Cause is that which helps the resulting into Effect. Or thiswise:—The Material Cause is that inevitable antecedent state adequate to effectuate the immediate consequent state; as illustrated by the consequent state of being the jar effected from the antecedent state of being the clod of earth. The Effective Cause is that which is required to be different from the modification (or the modifying). In this case the Instrumental Cause is included in the Effective (cause). Whichever be the position adopted, the three-foldness or the two-foldness of the Cause, the characteristics of Cause is evident, and this is found in the (Prime) Cause of the Universe, the Blessed All-God (*Bhagavān Nārāyaṇa*).

If it be asked how in Nārāyaṇa rests (or abides) the (ultimate) causality, the reply is:—Such conclusion is arrived at after an examination of all the Vedānta Texts (bearing on the question), rationally argued out. Thus: To begin with, matter cannot be the Cause of the Universe, for it is devoid of thinking[264] *etc.* In the Chhāndogya (-Upanishat) however, that which is indicated by the terms: *Sat*, *Ākāśa* (Ether), *Prāṇa*, is seen to be (stated as) the Cause of the Universe. In the Vājasaneyaka (Up°), the term *Brahman* is discovered (to be so). By the canon known as the 'resultant import of all the branches (of the Veda)',[265] all the texts which relate to Cause (of the Universe) must be interpreted to signify one Specific Object. Hence terms of general import such as *Sat* (Being) *etc.*, must ultimately connote the specific Brahman, according to the (analogical) rule of 'goat-animal'.[266] In the manner

[264] Read [*Vedānta-Sūtras* I. 1. 5]: *Īkshater nâ 'śabdam.* Thinking or mind.

[265] Known as the *sarva-śakhā-pratyaya-nyāya.*

[266] Known as the *Chāga-paśu-nyāya*, which means that when an animal is mentioned as eligible for sacrifice, the question necessarily arises as to what animal is particularly meant. 'Goat' is the answer, which is decisive. Hence general terms such as *sat etc.*, find their ultimate decisive significance in a definite (specific) term, which is found to be Nārāyaṇa, by an examination of the various generic terms bearing on the subject and which are scattered in various parts of the Veda.

aforesaid, the term Brahman is next circumscribable into the (more specific) term *Ātman* found in the Aitareya (-Upanishat). What then is indicated by this term *Ātman*,—the Vedic celebrity Indra? Or Agni, of similar report? Or Sūrya, known as the adorable? Or Soma, said to be the Cause? Or Kubera, known to be the bestower of whatever is desired? Or Yama? Or Varuṇa? When such doubt arises, they (deities or demigods) may be disposed of as incapable of being the Cause of the Universe, by reason of their being known to be subject to *karma* and possessed of limited affluence.

But in the Śvetāśvatara (-Upanishat), it is apparent that Śiva is (stated to be) the Cause (of the Universe). Similarly in the Atharva-Śikhā (-Upanishat), the entity designated Śambhu is mentioned as the object of adoration and as Cause. Likewise in the Atharva-Śiras (-Upanishat), the entity designated as Rudra is stated to be the Soul of all (things). And in the Taittirīya, Hiraṇya-garbha is mentioned as the Cause of the Universe. In all these cases, applying the canon (of interpretation) known as the 'Generic-Specific (*sāmānya-viśesha-nyāya*), the fact of the general terms Śiva, Śambhu and Rudra finding their specific significance in Hiraṇyagarbha will be clear. Again if the radical (or etymological) sense of the term Śiva be considered, it means *well* or *good* (or *auspicious*) as may be seen from the usages: 'Let it be *well* with all the Universe', 'Let the deed be *good*', 'Let thy path be *good*' *etc.* Similarly Rudra signifies Agni-(fire). Hence, judged by the etymological force of such common terms as Maheśvara, Śambhu *etc.*, they find their particular significance in the Fourfaced (entity, Hiraṇyagarbha).

But a protest may be entered why the terms Śiva *etc.*, referred to as the Cause (of the Kosmos) should not through their primary significance, (be construed to) indicate Rudra? This cannot be done, inasmuch as the origination of Rudra (Śiva) is narrated (in the Scriptures) as happening from the Four-faced (Demiurge), and Rudra is not free from (the taints of) sin; and therefore cannot constitute the Cause, (of the Universe). Hence terms such as Śiva *etc.*, receive their ultimate connotation as the Four-faced, severally designated as Hiraṇyagarbha, Prajāpati, Svayambhūḥ *etc.*,[267]

By a similar ratiocination, the terms Svayambhūḥ, Hiraṇyagarbha and Prajāpati may be traced up to (the Ultimate Source) Nārāyaṇa, for Nārāyaṇa, as the Supreme Cause, as the Being that all terms connote, as the Saviour (*moksha-prada*), as the Kosmos-bodied *etc.*, is proved in the Mahopanishat, Nārāyaṇ-opanishat, Subāl-opanishat, Maitrāyaṇīya (-Upaṇishat), Purusha-sūkta, Nārāyaṇâ- 'nuvāka, Antaryāmi-Brāhmaṇa *etc.* Hence Nārāyaṇa alone is the Cause of all the Kosmos, and the Knowable of all sciences.

No doubt need arise that the Science (of God) called the *Antar-āditya-vidyā* may relate to Rudra, for from a majority of authorities (Scriptures), it is proved that it relates to Vishṇu. The term *Bharga* is not to be understood as (a masculine-indicating) termination: A (अ). Nor need a doubt arise that in the Science, *Dahara-vidyā*,

---

[267] See Indian Antiquary Vol. xxxix for Nov. 1910. viz., Piḷḷai Lokâ'cārya's *Rahasya*: 'Refugee's Refuge.'

the term *Ākāśa* implying Nārāyaṇa, has Rudra for its In-dwelling (*antaryāmi*), for the In-dwelling there referred to are the auspicious graces or perfections inhering in Nārāyaṇa. In this same way the interpretations of all the Sciences (*Vidyās*) may be conceived.[268]

The inference thus is that He who is possessed of all Holy Graces, Perfections, Glories, Who is distinct from matter (*prakṛti*) and soul (*purusha*), Who is constituted of these, the Supreme Brahman, *viz.*, Nārāyaṇa, is the Cause of the Kosmos.

But it may be alleged that according to the monistic (*advaita*) texts (of the Scriptures), Brahman alone is real and undifferentiated (= devoid of attributes); what is fancied in it (Brahman) as the 'being cognizer' (*subject*) and as the 'being cognized' (*object*) *etc.*, is illusory; Brahman (itself) in consequence of nescience (*avidyā*) revolves in material life (*samsāra*); the monistic knowledge gained from such texts as:

'That thou art'[269]

---

[268] See (my) *Bhagavad-Gītā* with *Rāmānujā's Commentary*, Table of the 32 *Vidyās*. Pp. 129-130

[269] '*Tat tvam asi Śvetaketo* ! &c' [*Chhāndogya-Up°* VI. 7 *ff*].

dispels it (i. e. *samsāra* or *avidyā*). When thus, views such as these held by other schools, go to establish the sense of the Vedānta (texts) to point to an undifferentiated Brahman, which is but consciousness absolute, how could they connote Nārāyaṇa, and the discourse (hold) that He is possessed of all the Holy Graces (or Excellent Attributes)? The reply to this is thus:—From the texts referring to the Cause (of the Universe), Nārāyaṇa has been shown as the Cause; the conflict that seems to exist between the dualistic and monistic texts is reconcilable by means of the reconciling (or arbitration, *ghaṭaka*) texts; the texts that seem to import non-differentiation (or quality-lessness) are interpretable as meaning absence of evil qualities; as there is no authority by which to suppose a nescience, consequent on which the notions 'cognizer' and the 'cognizer' come to be fancied, the Effect (generating) from Brahman is real; if by nescience, Brahman itself rolls into material life as Soul (*Jīva*), the faults pertaining to the Soul necessarily attach to Brahman, and no other agent (than Brahman) can be conceived as the banisher (of that material life). As therefore the contention of monism cannot be sustained, no undifferentiated Brahman, as but mere consciousness is established; *ergo*, Brahman is full of exquisite Graces, and is Nārāyaṇa, Who is the Source of the Kosmos, and Bestower of eternal bliss (*moksha*) *etc.*

Brahman, as constituted of the Subtle, Conscient (*cit*) and the Non-conscient (*acit*) alone is the Cause of the Kosmos; and as constituted of the Gross Conscient and Non-conscient, alone is the Effect. Thus the creed of the Viśishṭâdvaita Vedāntins is that no Cause is different from its Effect.[370]

As God (*Îśvara*) is admitted, the views of the

[370] This is the law of Correlation. Every Effect has its own antecedent Cause to which it is correlated as gross to subtle. This is also the great doctrine of Evolution (*pariṇāma-vāda*) which Rāmānuja formulates and emphasizes. What is the evolute but its evolvent itself manifested in a different mode. No teak tree can be a product of a banyan seed. The Vedāntic evolution is triform, i.e. of the whole Complex Entity: the Viśishṭa-Brahman, i.e. God-Soul-Matter, *vide* Pp: 49 *ff* of my *Vade Mecum of Vedānta.*

Schools of God-less Sāṅkhya, the Mīmāṁsakas *etc.*, are exploded. As Material Causality is predicated (by us) of this same (God), the views of the Schools of Yoga, Pāśupata and Naiyāyika are confuted, for their admission of God is confined to His Efficient Causation only.

In the same manner as Material as well as Efficient causation is ascribable to God, are ascribable to Him the faculties of action, stimulation, governance, illuminance, permission, succour, neutrality and so forth.

In the same manner as the imperfections (known as) childhood, youth *etc.*, pertain to the body (*śarīra*), not the body-holder (*śarīri*), the soul, so is it in the case of the All-Soul (Paramātman), the bodied of Soul *(cit)* and Non-soul *(acit)*. There is thus no conflict with the Śruti (Scriptures) which proclaims the unmodifiable (character of God). As a rule, what is cognised as 'body' in the world is what possesses the properties of being 'sustained' (*ādheyatva*), 'controlled' (*vidheyatva*), and 'subordinated' (*śeshatva*) (by Soul); the Kosmos is the 'body' of God; but the imperfections pertaining to the body do not effect Him.

This God *(Īśvara)* is infinitive *(vibhu)*. To be infinite is to be pervading. This (pervasion) is threefold: (1) By essence, (2) By attributive consciousness, (3) By representation *(vigraha)*. He is called boundless *(Ananta)*. Boundless means the negation of the three kinds of limitations. The three kinds of limitations are those (1) by space, (2) by time and (3) by thing.

The qualities of Truth *(satyatva)*, Holiness *(amalatva)*, Illimitability *(anantatva)*, betoken the essential nature of God; the qualities of Omniscience *(jñāna)*, Omnipotence *(śakti)* *etc.*, describe Him, on such (essential) characterisation. The qualities of Omniscience, Omnipotence *etc.*, are requisite for purposes of Creation. The qualities of Love, Meekness, Accessibility *etc.*, are requisite for suasion (to souls) to take shelter. The qualities of Mercy *etc.*, are useful for purposes of protection. The import of these qualities has been discussed in the Section on Consciousness, and no expatiation here is therefore called for.

This God first created the (Mundane) Egg; and then by His immanency in the Four-faced (*Caturmukha)*, Daksha, Time *etc.*, continues creation. He becomes the Protector by incarnating as Vishṇu, abiding in Manu, Time *etc.*, and directly Himself. He is Destroyer by His indwelling in Rudra, Time, the destroyer (Yama) *etc.* Hence He is the Creator, Protector and Destroyer.

God as thus depicted assumes five aspects: (1) *Para* or the Transcendent, (2) Vyūha or the Grouped, (3) *Vibhava* or the Incarnated, (4) *Antaryāmi* or the Immanent, and (5) *Archā* or the Imaged. The *Para* is Nārāyaṇa, variously called by the names Parabrahma *etc.*, Vāsudeva *etc.*, Who, four-armed, and beaming with His beatific presence, is exalted on the throne poised on its eight supports Dharma *etc.*, with Śesha over the seat, erected in the gemmed pavilion in the Divine Hall, guarded by the sentries: Caṇḍa, Pracaṇḍa, Bhadra, Subhadra, Jaya, Vijaya, Dhātṛi, Vidhātṛi *etc.*, in the Vaikunṭha-named-City of the Thrice-Magnificent Land,[271] protected

[271] Read: "*Tripādasyâ "mritam divi.*" [Purusha-sūkta].

by such city-keepers as Kumuda, Kamudāksha, Puṇḍarīka, Vāmana, Śaṅkukarṇa, Sarpanetra, Sumukha, Supratishṭha *etc.*, all divinely adorned and armed, with all the paraphernalia of servitors *etc*;—Who is supported by Śri, Bhū, Nīḷa *etc.*, armed with the divine weapons Conch, Discus *etc.*, decked with the divine ornaments Crown *etc.*,—Who is enjoyed by the 'Eternals': Ananta, Garuḍa, Vishvaksena *etc.*, ever chanting forth the Hymns of Sāma, and by other redeemed Souls (*mukta*)—and Who is the Home of all the countless Holy Graces: Wisdom, Power *etc.*[272] Vyūha (the Gregated or Grouped) is the fourfold aspect (of God) *viz.*, Vāsudeva, Saṅkarshaṇa, Pradyumna, and Aniruddha, designed for purposes of worship, creation of the worlds *etc.* Of these, Vāsudeva has the full complement of the Six Qualities; Saṅkarshana has Wisdom and Strength; Pradyumna has Wealth and Power; and Aniruddha Energy and Lustre; Thus are the (Six)

[272] See note 263. For all the descriptions here given the reader is referred to the oceanic literature known as the *Pāñcarātras*, (see JRAS for October 1911).

Qualities distributed. Each one of these four (aspects) hypostatize (*avatarati*) into three. They (thus) number twelve: Kešava *etc*; and they are the Presiding Deities of the twelve Suns of the twelve months. Their locations by vertical markings (on the body of the devotee) are fixed. Amongst them (twelve), Kešava is gold-coloured and wears four Discuses; Nārāyaṇa, dark-coloured, wears four Conches; Mādhava, gem-coloured, wears four Clubs; Govinda, moon-coloured, wears four Bows; Vishṇu, lotus-blossom-coloured, wears four Ploughs; Madhusūdana, lotus-coloured, wears four Maces; Trivikrama, fire-coloured, wears four Swords; Vāmana, young-Sun-coloured, wears four Vajras; Šrīdhara, lotus-coloured, wears four Shields; Hṛshīkeša, lightning-coloured, wears four Maces; Padmanābha, sun-coloured, wears the Five Weapons; Dāmodara, *indragopa*-coloured bears four Cords.

Vibhava or Incarnate Manifestation (or objectification) is the assumption (by God) of Forms resembling those of the Order (of Creation, in which He wills to appear). Ten of them are reckoned as by far the most renowned. They are the unique incarnations: the *Matsya*, the *Kūrma etc.* Of these the *Matsya* Incarnation was undertaken in order to overcome the Daityas who stole the Vedas, and restore them (viz., the Authority) to Brahmā. The *Kūrma* Incarnation was undertaken in order to extract ambrosia (*amṛta*), (from the Milk Sea), calculated to bestow (lasting) health and immortality on beings. The *Varāha* Incarnation was undertaken in order to raise His Consort (Earth from the ocean) that He may (thus) exemplify his power to) lift creatures drowned in the Ocean of worldliness (*samsāra*). The *Narasiṁha* Incarnation was undertaken with a view to protect his protege (Prahlāda) and kill the Asura (Hiraṇya-kaśipu),—by springing out of a pillar. The *Vāmana* Incarnation was undertaken in order to cleanse the worlds by means of water issuing from his lotus-feet (i.e. Gaṅgā), by the transfigured (from Vāmana) Trivikrama. The *Paraśurāma* Incarnation was taken for the purpose of exterminating the wicked Kshatriyas. The *Rāma* Incarnation was undertaken in order to establish the Law of Righteousness (*Dharma*). The *Balabhadra* and *Rāma* Incarnations were assumed in order to overthrow Pralamba *etc.* The *Kṛshṇa* Incarnation was donned with the object of pointing to men the Final Way (to blessedness).[273] The *Kalki* Incarnation is intended to put an end to the irreligious, and establish Righteousness in all its plenitude.[274] In this way, each one of these Ten Incarnations has countless varieties.

Padmanābha *etc.*, have also thirty-six ramifications. Again are there (varieties of manifestations) such as Dadhibhakta, Hayagrīva, Nara-Nārāyaṇa *etc.*

Likewise there are such other modal diversities as the Primary (*Mukhya*), Secondary (*Gauṇa*),

---

[273] Consult Bhagavad-Gītā, particularly xviii. 66 and the elaborate commentaries written thereon by the Ācāryas. This forms the third of the Rahasya-traya, which is one of the 18 Rahasyas by Piḷḷai Lokācārya, Nos. 1, 12, 13, and 17 in the list given on Page 570. JRAS. for July, 1910.

[274] Read *Vishṇu-Purāṇa*, *Rāmāyaṇa*, *Bhārata*, *Harivamśa*, *Bhāgavata* etc., for detailed accounts of all the Avatāras (Incarnations).

Full (*Pūrṇa*), Partial (*Aṁśa*), and Obsessing (*Āveśa*). Amongst these, the distinction of Worshippable and Non-worshippable must be borne in mind.

The reason for incarnating, is (God's own) Will, not Karma.* As for the *motif* (for incarnating), it is to protect the good, by destroying the wicked.

The Immanent phase is that of abidance in the regions of the heart of the Soul through all its states of experience in heavens, hells *etc.*, as the Souls' (constant) Friend, and realisable by Yogis. Though co-dwelling with the Soul (Easternal Partner), He is intact of taints affecting it.

The Image-Incarnation is the species of Forms presented (for worship), in homes, hamlets, cities, selected hills *etc.*, devoid of distances interposed by space and time; deigning to descend with His immaterial (i.e., spiritual) Person into any material substance as may lovingly be chosen by

* I. e,, a necessitation contingent on the performance of an interested deed, but no such interestedness of a selfish character can abide in the Deity. Hence His Incarnations emanate from a perfectly Free Will.

the votary; lending Himself to the sweet will of His worshipper in all details (of worship such as) bath, food, place and rest; All-forgiving; the All-sufficient God! Four varieties of this (aspect) exist viz., Self-manifest *(Svayam-Vyakta)*, Superhuman or Celestial *(Daiva)*, Saint-made *(Saiddha)* and Man-made *(Mānusha)*.[278]

In all the Quintuple Hypostases aforesaid, God is ever present with Śrī (or Grace, His Consort). So Śruti and other Authorities declare. And therefore the view of those one-sided partisans who contend for Śrī-lessness, is exploded. (The Category of) God has thus been propounded.

Thus ends Advent IX,
The treatment of God (*Īśvara*)
in the
"Light of the School of Rāmānuja."

---

[278] See the Quinary Group, I. *Para-svarūpa*, Pp. 576-7. *Artha-Pañcaka*, in JRAS, for July, 1910.

ADVENT X.

THE NON-SUBSTANCE (*Adravya*).

After the treatment thus given to (the Category) Substance (*Dravya*), that of non-substance will now be taken up.

Non-substance is divisible into ten classes only *viz.* :—(1, 2, 3), the pure, motile or motive and dark (qualities inherent in matter), (4, 5, 6, 7, 8), Sound, Touch, Colour, Savour, Odour, (9) conjunction (*Saṁyoga*), and (10) Force (*Śakti*).

Satva or Pureness is the non-Substance (or Quality) which is the root-cause of brightness, happiness, buoyancy *etc.*, non-sensible, and other than force *etc.* It is of two kinds : Absolute Pureness (*Śuddha-satva*) and mixed or Alloyed Pureness (*Miśra-satva*). Absolute Pureness is the Pureness inherent in Substance, devoid from restlessnessness (*Rajas*) and darkness (*Tamas*). This (exists) in the Eternal Expanse (i. e. Spiritual Regions). Metaphorically (or secondarily) it is ascribed to God

(*Īsvara*), its Initiator. The Mixed Pureness is so called by reason of the association of pureness with restlessnessness and darkness. This pervades the Triune (=matter) and is tropically (or secondarily) attributed to the soul (*Jīva*) consorting with it (matter).

Rajas or restlessness is the non-Substance (or Quality), which is the root-cause of passion, desire, greed, activity *etc.*, non-sensible and other than force *etc.*

Tamas, darkness (or Dross) is the non-Substance (or Quality), which is the root-cause of infatuation, inattention, listlessness *etc.*, non-sensible and other than force *etc.*

These three (qualities) permeate matter conterminously; adhere to the soul (which is) in bondage with matter; non-eternal; constantly fluxing; equipoised in the state of Dissolution (*pralaya*); agitated in the state of Creation (*sṛshṭi*); useful for the processes of Creation, Continuance and Dissolution; and are the cause of the mutual contrarieties existing (in the Universe) determined by the dispensations or bent of God's Will. These (properties) are common (to this

Triad). (The *differentiæ* are):—The *Satva* Quality is the cause of blessedness born of lucid knowledge *etc.*, and productive of Redemption (*moksha*). The *Rajas* Quality is the cause of pain *etc.*, born of attachment &c., begot by *karma,** and the means of bringing the supra-mundane (fruits) such as *Svarga*, *Naraka*, etc. The *Tamas* Quality is the cause of ignorance, lethargy *etc.*, and productive of Damnation (*naraka*). Hence Satva *etc.*, are Qualities; and not possessed of the characteristics of Substance.

Sound which abides in all the Five Elements is that which we cognize by the sense of hearing. It is of two descriptions: articulate aad non-articulate. The Fifty Letters (of the alphabet), A, K, C, Ṭ, T, P, Y, *etc.*, comprise the articulate (sound), and this is utterable by means of the palate *etc.*, by gods, men *etc.* The non-articulate (sound) is such as that emanating from a drum

---

* The Law of Action and Re-action. On the moral plane it is the Nemesis or the Law of Retribution. When this Law is transcended, the state is that of Redemption (*Moksha*).

etc. By the ear is sound, so described, apprehensible. Either by the sense (of hearing) emanant, or the excitative air vibrant, is sound perceived. But Scriptures speak of sound as Substance; how then can it be non-substance (i. e. quality)? The escape (from this objection) consists in showing that the composition of *Praṇava* (*Aum*) by its components A (अ) *etc.*, is made through what is signified (by A *etc.*, viz; *Ākāśa*).[276]

Touch is that Quality which we perceive by the sense of touch (in skin), other and separate (than those of the other senses). This is of three kinds: cold, warm and equable (tem-

---

[276] Though as a constituent part in a compound, and as cause to an effect, the constituent may bear the semblance of a substance, yet the fact that the constituent is so by means of its origin from, or dependency on, a medium makes it partake the characteristic of a non-substance, as for example, the sound A, though a material (or substantial) cause to produce Aum the effect, it is a quality by reason of its origination from, or dependency on, the substance Akāśa or Ether. The significant (*vācaka*) is A, the signified (*vākya*) by that significant is Ether, of which the significant in the present case is as quality or attribute to substance.

perature). The cold touch is (perceivable) in water, the warm in fire, the equable in earth and air. Also it (touch) is divisible into what is modified, or effected (a product—*pākaja*) and what is unmodified or uneffected (causal or elementary *a-pākaja*). The former is in earth; the latter is in the other three (viz., ether, fire and water). The touch pertaining in a special manner, to (such things as) nectar, poison, pearl, silk, stone, cow, Brāhmaṇa, Caṇḍāla[271] *etc.*, is classifiable under the head 'effected.'

---

[271] Physically, any combination or integration brought about by natural agencies, chiefly by fire, is a product. The quality of touch undergoes change by these processes. These maturatory physical processes, carry with them moral or spiritual consequences *pari-passu*. Thus a *Caṇḍāla* is a low-caste personage. He becomes the 'untouchable' because he has so become by all the modifications produced by conditions such as natal, sacramental, social and moral; and the environments comprised of loathsome habits in food, drink, and marriage. If according to *Matthew ix. 20, 21*, a woman touching the hem of Jesus is sanctified, there is meaning in the doctrine that touching unclean objects contacts pollution. There is *physical* as well as *moral* contagion according to Brāhmanic doctrines.

Colour is that Quality which is perceived by our sense of sight (eye) alone, other and separate (than the other qualities). It is of four kinds: white, red, yellow and dark. White of varieties is the colour found in silver, conch, shell, moon *etc.* Red of varieties is found in fire, rose, pomegranate, *bandhu-jīva*,[278] coral, ruby *etc.* Yellow of varieties is the colour found in gold, saffron, turmeric *etc.* Dark of varieties is the colour found in sapphire, bee, cloud, night (or darkness), *tamāla*,[279] grass *etc.* Some, following the Śruti [280], hold the view that yellow is a species of red. As an alternative (classification), colour is twofold: radiant and non-radiant. Radiant is (what is found) in (self-) luminous (objects); the non-radiant is (what is found) in

[278] '*Pentapetes Phœnicea*, a plant with a red flower which opens at midday and withers away the next morning at sunrise.' [Monier Williams' Saṁskṛt-English Dictionary].

[279] *Xanthochymus Pictorius.*

[280] *I. e.*, according to the passage in the Chhāṇḍogya-Upanishat, vi. 4. 1; '*Yad agne rohitam rūpam tejasas tad rūpam tacchuklaṁ tad apāṁ yat kṛshṇam tad annasya.*'

such (things) as the eye, water, *etc.* Thus four-fold is colour, and therefore the view some maintain that there is a fifth colour the variegated, is rejected. For reasons similar, the idea that there is a variegated odour, touch and savour, is debarred.

Savour is the Quality perceptible to our sense of taste (tongue), other and of different species (than the rest of the qualities). It is of six kinds; sweet, sour, saline, bitter, pungent, and astringent. The sweet varieties are of (such articles as) sugar-cane, milk, sugar *etc.* The sour varieties are of the mango, tamarind, myrobalan-fruit *etc.* The saline varieties are of salt, saline products *etc.* The bitter varieties are of *kiṁpāka*,[281] margosa *etc.* The pungent varieties are of ginger, pepper, mustard *etc.* The astringent varieties are of the yellow myrobalan (gallnut) *vibhītaki*, [282] mango-sprout *etc.*

Odour is the Quality apprehensible by our sense of smell (nose), other and of a different order (than the other qualities). It is of two

[281] *Trichosanthes Palmata*, also *Cucumis Colocynthus.*

[282] *Terminalia Belerica.*

kinds: odour and mal-odour. The varieties of odour (or fragrance) are of sandal, musk, saffron, *campaka*[283] *etc.* The mal-odours are what may be found in others than these. Odour is specifically of the earth, and varieties spring out of its modifications. The perception of odour in air, water *etc.*, is by reason of its impregnation with earth and is tropically so (used) like the expression 'iron burns.'[284] Though all qualities may abide in all the elements in virtue of their (elements') quintuplicity, (the assignment of) particular qualities (to particular elements) is by reason of (their) predominancy. There is thus no contradiction. The change of quality, consequent on maturation, (or modification a substance may undergo) occurs in its own sub-stratum (i.e. in the same substance). When this (change) is explicable by the non-disappearance of its own substratum, the tenet that the atoms (themselves) undergo change is untenable.[285]

---

[283] *Michelia Champaka.*

[284] It is the fire that burns, but tropically (or metaphorically) the burning is imputed to iron.

[285] The *Vaiśeshika* School thinks that heat acts on the atoms composing a jar, atoms change, and hence

Conjunction (*Saṁyoga*) is the (Quality which is the) cause of the cognition of the conjunct (objects). This quality is universal to the Six Substances.[286]

The contradiction of its non-existence as well as existence in the substratum, is accountable by the fact of the substratum having diverse parts.[287] Conjunction (a Quality) is both of the non-eternal and of the eternal character. The former (subsists) in limited (objects) by the impulse of both the 'conjunct' (objects) as two goats or two duellists (rushing towards each other for combat), or by the impulse of one, as of a hawk perching on a post.[287] Some talk of a Conjunction

---

qualities change; whereas the Nayyāyika School thinks that it is otherwise. The former are known as the *Pīlu-pāka-vādins*, the latter *Piṭhara-pāka-vādins*. [See *Tarka-Saṁgraha-Dīpikā*, I].

[286] Consult Advent IV. The Six Substances are, (1) Matter, (2) Time, (3) Pure Matter, (4) Attributive Consciousness, (5) Soul, (6) God. Cohesion, Adhesion, Molecular, Magnetic, Chemical *etc.*, attraction may all be grouped under this Quality.

[287] For example, if a bird is perched on the top of a steeple, the conjunction of the bird with the steeple exists at the top which is a part of the steeple

originating from a Conjunction, for example the conjunction of a book with the body, arising from its (book's) conjunction with the hand; but we say no, inasmuch as one conjunction—hand with book—implies the other, and no two successive conjunctions, therefore, one springing from the other (need predication). For similar reasoning, the origination of a Disjunction from another Disjunction is also discarded. Disjunction *(Vibhāga* or *Viyoga)* is none other than the negation of Conjunction of bodies; hence it is not a distinct Quality. The Eternal (kind of) Conjunction is between infinite *(vibhu)* substances. Conjunction of eternal (*lit.* non-originated = *aja*) substances, is admitted by Śruti (Vedas); by Inference also the Conjunction of eternal substances is establishable thus:—

'An infinite substance has conjunction with an infinite substance,

For it is substance,

Like the jar'; (or),

---

and not exists at its bottom, which is its (steeple's) another part.

'An infinite substance is conjoined with God (*Īśvara*),

For it is substance,

Like the jar'; (or),

'God (*Īśvara*) is conjoined with Time *etc.*,

For He is substance,

Like the jar.'

By such (ratiocinations), the Conjunction of infinite substances is stablished.[288]

Now, Force is that particular non-Substance (i. e. Quality) which stands as the reason of all causation. This is made evident both by Infer-

---

[288] An objection is raised; how can two or more infinites be conjoined, inasmuch as conjunction implies partition; but when there is partition or division, the substance cannot be infinite? This objection is met by saying that infinites are eternally conjoined and never brought about in time, and hence possible; and this is supported by the Revelations (Śruti). The conjunction therefore is of the metaphysical, ideal, or spiritual description, and therefore bears no analogy to physical or spatial conjunctions, except the mere fact of conjunction. What is meant is the co-substantiality of infinites; that is, two or more infinites can co-exist, their infinitiveness remaining unaffected.

ence as well as Scriptures (*Āgama*). That Force (or Power) which is not palpable to the senses, is that by which fire ceases to burn when obstructed by the presence of such things as gems, charms *etc.*, though there is no paucity of substance to help its nature (i. e., help fire to burn). The existence of such (power) is evident in the magnet. This power abides in (all) the Six Substances.[289] The abidance (of Force) in God (*Bhagavān*) is stablished by the 'Gem-Purāṇa' (=*Vishṇu Purāṇa*) *etc.* Hence the Quality known as Force (or Power) is discoverable universally.

But if it be asked how when Qualities have been enumerated as Twenty-four,[290] only Ten

---

[289] *I.e.*, (1) Matter, (2) Time, (3) Pure Matter, (4) Attributive Consciousness, (5) Soul, (6) God. [See Advent IV].

[290] The Sixteen according to *Tarka-Saṁgraha* are:—(1) Colour, (2) Savour, (3) Odour, (4) Touch, (5) Number, (6) Extension, (7) Severalty, (8) Conjunction, (9) Disjunction, (10) Priority, (11) Posteriority, (12) Gravity, (13) Fluidity, (14) Viscidity, (15) Sound, (16) Thought, (17) Pleasure, (18) Pain, (19) Desire, (20) Aversion, (21) Will, (22) Virtue, (23) Vice, (24) Faculty.

have been recognised, the reply is: that as already shown, the Six (Qualities) Thought, Pleasure, Pain, Desire, Aversion and Will (or Effort) are but states of Consciousness—qualities or attributes of the Soul (*Jivâ-"tmā*). Virtue and Vice, contingent (respectively) on the Grace and Wrath of God, are resolvable into the Consciousness of God. The Power of Imagination is resolvable into a state of Consciousness, the Power of Momentum is accountable from the cause of Momentum (Energy), and the Power of Elasticity is accounted for by means of Conjunction. The Five (Qualities), Sound, Touch, Colour, Savour, and Odour are admitted as evident to the senses. Disjunction and Severalty are resolvable into the Negation of Conjunction. Priority and Posteriority are accountable by particularities of Space and Time. Number, Extension, Fluidity and Viscidity are accountable by the very nature of the substances to which they pertain. Gravity is properly resolvable into Force. Hence (the analysis of Non-Substance into) Ten, accords with reason.

Amongst these, Pureness, Restlessness and Darkness,—the Qualities of Matter,—are also (by attribution) Qualities of the Soul. But expressions like: 'Knowledge of the pure sort (*satva-rūpam jñānam*), 'Pure is the time' (*sātvikaḥ-kālaḥ*) *etc.*, are, on account of accident (*upādhi*), of a metaphorical description.

The Five—Sound etc., pertaining to matter, are well known as the Qualities of the Five Elements. The Absolutely Pure Matter of course (as shown in Advent VI) exists in the Eternal Expanse (=Spiritual Universe), and in God who is its Actuator (Will).

Conjunction and Force are universal (or common) to the Six Substances (*note* 286). Such is the distribution.

Non-Substance has thus been demonstrated.

Thus ends Advent X,
The Treatment of Non-Substance (*A-dravya*).
in the
'Light of the School of Rāmānuja'.

CONCLUSION.

In the aforesaid manner, have Principles (*arthas*) been expounded in this exegetic treatise on the Śārīraka* based on the works, composed by the ancient Ācāryas for the enlightenment of novices (in the science), i.e., these (works), viz:—

1. Dramiḍa-Bhāshya (by Dramiḍa-cārya).
2. Nyāya-Siddhi (by Nātha-muni if it is same as Nyāya-Tattva ?)
3. Siddhi-Traya (by Yāmuna-"cārya)
4. Śrī-Bhāshya (by Śrī Rāmānuja)
5. (Vedānta-) Dīpa (by do.)
6. (Vedānta-) Sāra (by do.)
5. (Vedārtha-) Saṁgraha (by do.)
8. Bhāshya-Vivaraṇa (by Eṅgaḷ-āzhvān or Vishṇu-citta)
9. Saṅgati-Mālā (by do. do.)
10. Shaḍartha-Saṁkshepa (by Somāśiy-āṇḍān =Somayāji-āndān or Rāmamiśra)
11. Śruta-prakāśikā (by Sudarśana-"cārya)

---

* See notes 10 and 153.

12. Tattva-Ratnākara (by Kūratt-āzhvān or Kūranātha)
13. Prajñā-Paritrāṇa (by Varada-Nārāyaṇa Bhaṭṭāraka)
14. Prameya-Saṁgraha (by do do.)
15. Nyāya-Kuliśa (by Vādihaṁsa-'mbuvāha or Kiḍāmbi Rāmānuja-p-piḷḷān) *
16. Nyāya-Sudarśana (by do.)
17. Darśana-Yāthātmya-Nirṇaya or Māna-Yāthātmya-Nirṇaya. (by Varada-Vishṇu-Miśra)
18. Tattva-Dīpa (by Vādikesari Saumyajā-mātṛī-Muni)
19. Tattva-Nirṇaya (by do.)
20. Sarvārtha-Siddhi (by Vedānta-"cārya)
21. Nyāya-Pariśuddhi (by do.)
22. Nyāya-Siddhāñjana (by do.)
23. Paramata-Bhaṅga (by do.)
24. Tattva-traya-Cuḷaka (by do.)
25. Tattva-Nirūpaṇa (by Vādikeśari Saumya-jāmātṛ-Muni)

---

* Appiḷḷār, *vide* 'Pazha-naḍai Viḷakkam' by Aṇṇā Appaṅgār.

26. Tattva-traya + (its) Vyākhyāna (by Piḷḷai Lokâcārya + Yatīndra-pravaṇa)
27. Caṇḍa-Māruta (by Śri Mahâ-"cārya* of Śoḷiṅgipura.)
28. Vedānta-Vijaya (by do.)
29. Pārāśarya-Vijaya (by do.) *etc.*

The Science of Spirit is concerned with the treatment of *Tattva* or (Final) Truth, *Hita* or Means, and *Purushārtha* or Goal. In this Summary of that Science, an investigation has been made, in the Sections on 'Matter', 'Soul' and 'God' of the *Truth*; † in the Section on 'Consciousness,' of the *Means*; in the Section on 'Eternal Universe' of the *Goal*. Hence it is clear that all the (Three): 'Truth,' 'Means' and 'Goal' have been dealt with. (Some) sages aver that there is One Truth (Verity or Category). The Ṛshis (Prophets) assert it as Two,—of the divisions Soul and Non-soul. The Ācāryas (Teachers) predicate Three, in pursuance of the Śruti (Scriptures) viz., the Enjoyed (matter), the Enjoyer (soul) and Ruler

* See Preface p. iii *ff*.

† The Three Primary Data (see Preface p. xix.)

(God). Some Ācāryas prefer to think a four-fold division, viz., (1) The Base or Evil (*Heya*), (2) its Remedy, (3) the Worthy (*Upādeya*), (4) its Means.[291] Other Leaders predicate it as Five-fold: viz., the Goal, the Seeker, the Means, the Fruit, the Bar.[292] Other Guides add Relation and delineate it (*Tattva*) as Six-fold.[293] Diversity of discussion does not point to diversity in the

---

[291] *I.E.* the (1) Sense-kingdom, (2) How to overcome it, the (3) Spirit-kingdom, (4) How to win it.

[292] See *Artha-Pañcaka*, or The Five Truths, JRAS for July, 1910.

[293] *I.E.* the disquisition into the nature of the relations subsisting between Matter, Soul and Spirit. Consult work No 10 *supra*. The relation is particularly that intimate, inalienable and indiscerptible one subsisting between the Kosmos as the body (*Śarira*) and Nārāyaṇa as the Bodied (*Śarīri*), the very connotation of this term being the Spirit (*Śarīri*) enlivening or informing that body (*Śarīra*). All the other relations amongst Godhood, Soulhood etc., are contingent thereon. The relations between God (Spirit) and Soul are grouped under Nine Heads, see Piḷḷai Lokâ-"cārya's Rahasya No. 11: *Nava-vidha-sambandha* [P. 570, Artha-Pañcaka, JRAS, July 1910]. Śri-Rāmâyaṇa is an exegesis on these relations.

subject-matter, forasmuch as it is due to such view being determined by differentiæ in the characterisation. Hence the whole (subject) is clear.

Quintessentially, the purport of the Vedāntas is that there is but one Secondless Truth (God) constitutive of the Conscient (Soul) and the Non-Conscient (Matter)—the Brahman. Hence cognising this Conscient-and-Non-Conscient-adjectivated Brahman as the One Unity, the Blessed Bādarāyaṇa (i. e. Kṛshṇa-Dvaipāyana-Vyāsa) started the inquiry:

'Now, then, the investigation into Brahman,'[294] and closed it by showing Its (the Unit Brahman's) qualified (or predicated) nature.

Therefore, Nārāyaṇa is the Predicated of the Conscient and the Non-Conscient,—designated Brahman,—named Vishṇu,—the Supreme Vāsudeva.

What the Tenets (or System) of the School of the Viśishṭā-'dvaitins[295] are, is thus evident.

---

[294] *Athā-'to Brahma-jijñāsā* [Vedānta-Sūtras, I-1-1].

[295] The conception of God according to the Viśishṭā-'dvaita School as evident from this closing

Thus ends the Conclusion
of the 'Light of the School of Rāmānujā'
Composed by
Šrīnivāsā-"cārya, the First Disciple of
Šrīman-Mahā-"cārya
of the Holy Line of the Vādhūlas.

Iti vividha vicitram māna-meya-prakāšam
Ghana-guruvara-dāsen'-oktam ādāya šāstrāt,
Yatipati-mata-dīpam Veda-Vedānta-sāram
Sa bhavati matimān yas sat-kaṭāksh-aika-
lakshyaḥ.

GLORY TO RĀMĀNUJA.

---

sentence is that of a living, loving, personal God in the closest intimacy with His Creation consisting of both Conscient (*cit*) as well as Non-Conscient (*acit*) elements.